THE POWER OF GOD

LIBRARY OF LIVING FAITH

JOHN M. MULDER, General Editor

THE POWER
OF GOD

by

DANIEL L. MIGLIORE

THE WESTMINSTER PRESS
PHILADELPHIA

Copyright © 1983 Daniel L. Migliore

Scripture quotations from the Revised Standard Version of the
Bible are copyrighted 1946, 1952, ©1971, 1973 by the Division of
Christian Education of the National Council of the Churches of
Christ in the U.S.A., and are used by permission.

Acknowledgment is made to the following for permission to use
copyrighted material:

Georges Borchardt, Inc., for excerpt from "Power and Love," from
Martin Buber, *A Believing Humanism* (Simon and Schuster), tr. by
Maurice Feldman; copyright © 1967 by Maurice Feldman.

Houghton Mifflin Company, for excerpt from Archibald Mac-
Leish, *J.B.: A Play in Verse.* Copyright ©1956, 1957, 1958 by
Archibald MacLeish.

Harold Ober Associates Incorporated, for excerpt from "Poem for
Rich Churches," by Langston Hughes, in Jean Wagner, *Les Poèts
Nègres des États-Unis* (Paris: Librairie Istra, 1963). Copyright ©
1963. All rights reserved.

First edition

Published by The Westminster Press®
Philadelphia, Pennsylvania

PRINTED IN THE UNITED STATES OF AMERICA
9 8 7 6 5 4 3 2 1

Library of Congress Cataloging in Publication Data

Migliore, Daniel L., 1935–
    The power of God.

    (Library of living faith)
    Bibliography: p.
    1. Providence and government of God. 2. Power
(Christian theology) I. Title. II. Series.
BT96.2.M53 1983   231.7   82-20037
ISBN 0-664-24454-8 (pbk.)

FOR REBECCA AND MARK

We cannot avoid
Using Power,
Cannot escape the compulsion
To afflict the world,
So let us, cautious in diction,
And mighty in contradiction,
Love powerfully.

Martin Buber,
"Power and Love"

CONTENTS

FOREWORD

The word "theology" comes from two Greek words—*theos* ("God") and *logos* ("word" or "thought"). Theology is simply words about God or thinking about God. But for many Christians, theology is remote, abstract, baffling, confusing, and boring. They turn it over to the professionals—the theologians—who can ponder and inquire into the ways of God with the world.

This series, Library of Living Faith, is for those Christians who thought theology wasn't for them. It is a collection of ten books on crucial doctrines or issues in the Christian faith today. Each book attempts to show why our theology—our thoughts about God—matters in what we do and say as Christians. The series is an invitation to readers to become theologians themselves—to reflect on the Bible and on the history of the church and to find their own ways of understanding the grace of God in Jesus Christ.

The Library of Living Faith is in the tradition of another series published by Westminster Press in the 1950s, the Layman's Theological Library. This new collection of volumes tries to serve the church in the challenges of the closing decades of this century.

The ten books are based on the affirmation of the Letter to the Ephesians (4:4–6): "There is one body and one Spirit, just as you were called to the one hope that belongs to your call, one Lord, one faith, one baptism, one God and

Father of us all, who is above all and through all and in all."
Each book addresses a particular theme as part of the
Christian faith as a whole; each book speaks to the church
as a whole. Theology is too important to be left only to the
theologians; it is the work and witness of the entire people
of God.

But, as Ephesians says, "grace was given to each of us
according to the measure of Christ's gift" (Eph. 4:7), and
the Library of Living Faith tries to demonstrate the diversity of theology in the church today. Differences, of course,
are not unique to American Christianity. One only needs to
look at the New Testament and the early church to see how
"the measure of Christ's gift" produced disagreement and
conflict as well as a rich variety of understandings of
Christian faith and discipleship. In the midst of the unity of
the faith, there has never been uniformity. The authors in
this series have their own points of view, and readers may
argue along the way with the authors' interpretations. But
each book presents varying points of view and shows what
difference it makes to take a particular theological position.
Sparks may fly, but the result, we hope, will be a renewed
vision of what it means to be a Christian exhibiting in the
world today a living faith.

These books are also intended to be a library—a set of
books that should be read together. Of course, not everything is included. As the Gospel of John puts it, "There are
also many other things which Jesus did; were every one of
them to be written I suppose that the world itself could not
contain the books that would be written" (John 21:25).
Readers should not be content to read just the volume on
Jesus Christ or on God or on the Holy Spirit and leave out
those on the church or on the Christian life or on Christianity's relationship with other faiths. For we are called to one
faith with many parts.

The volumes are also designed to be read by groups of
people. Writing may be a lonely task, but the literature of

the church was never intended for individuals alone. It is for the entire body of Christ. Through discussion and even debate, the outlines of a living faith can emerge.

Daniel L. Migliore is Professor of Systematic Theology at Princeton Theological Seminary, where he has taught since 1962. He is the author of *Called to Freedom: Liberation Theology and the Future of Christian Doctrine* (Westminster, 1980), as well as many articles and reviews. An ordained minister in the United Presbyterian Church, Dr. Migliore is a graduate of Westminster College in Pennsylvania, Princeton Theological Seminary, and Princeton University.

When asked why he wrote this book, he replied: "This topic is at the heart of our most fundamental theological, moral, and social problems today. The question of the power of God and the question of the proper exercise of human power are very closely related. The power of God made known decisively in Jesus Christ, the crucified and living Lord, is neither sheer almightiness nor mere impotence; it is power that makes for freedom, justice, and lasting community. The gospel of God's power brings not only a word of judgment but also offers new life and hope to both the 'powerful' and the 'powerless' of our age."

For some people, God may be distant and unreal, but in this book Dr. Migliore offers an understanding of God that is rooted in the experience of people who know suffering, despair, and persecution, as well as joy, faith, and hope. It is a book for people who know life, and it shows how God in Christ makes life more abundant.

JOHN M. MULDER

Louisville Presbyterian Theological Seminary
Louisville, Kentucky

1
THE QUESTION
OF GOD'S POWER

Our Experience of Power and Powerlessness

People ask about God for many reasons. Some ask out of curiosity, others out of habit, still others because they remember how important belief in God was for their parents or grandparents. Most people, however, ask about God out of a sense of urgency. They seek the deepest and surest foundation for life in a world filled with both promise and peril.

Even if neglected or avoided for a time, the question about God never entirely dies out. That is because it has its roots in everyday human experience. The question of God is not a purely academic question but a profoundly practical question; it arises not at the periphery but at the very center of our common human life.

When people ask about God, they seldom want to know answers to questions such as whether God's existence can be proved. Many philosophers and theologians, of course, like to ask that sort of question. They spend a great amount of time and effort debating proofs for or against the existence of God. Such debates, however, are far removed from the concrete life situations in which most people ask about God.

The question of God arises out of the restless and searching human heart. It often takes the form of a cry that

comes, as the psalmist says, "out of the depths" (Ps. 130:1).
Men and women are moved to raise the question of God by
their everyday life, by their common human experiences of
power and powerlessness. They ask about God because
they look for a life-giving power beyond themselves. They
seek a transforming power that makes for wholeness and
fulfillment of life in the midst of their brokenness and
emptiness. They seek a power that works for freedom,
justice, and peace in a world spoiled by bondage, injustice,
and hatred. They raise the question of God as they experience many relentless forces bearing down upon them and
as they recognize the limitations of their own powers.

Consider a few examples. A woman lies awake in her
hospital room in the middle of the night. She knows she has
an incurable cancer. During the last few weeks, she has had
a lot of time to think—about herself, about her family, about
her work, about the meaning of life. She is frightened, as
never before, by her sense of helplessness. Until recently,
she had always been in control of her life, a person who
took charge of things. Many people depended on her
seemingly endless vitality and strength. Not an especially
religious person, she now raises questions that she never
considered very important before. In the stillness of her
hospital room she wonders: "God, do you really care for
me? Can I count on you to help me in the difficult days
ahead?"

In an inner-city church a young black pastor sits at his
desk and ponders what he will say to his congregation on
Sunday morning. Most of his people are unemployed. Their
hope for a new and better life is vanishing. They are weary
of fighting city hall about the wretched housing conditions
and the pathetic schools in the community. Whenever the
pastor looks from the pulpit at the faces of his people, he
sees the years—the centuries—of suffering and powerlessness. In this situation of misery and despair, the pastor is
moved to question God. "Do you really care for these poor

and oppressed people? Don't you see that they are being destroyed by their powerlessness?"

Whether sick or healthy, man or woman, black, brown, or white, most of us could recognize something universally human in both of these situations. However powerful we may imagine ourselves to be, all of us, like the hospitalized woman, eventually come up against the limits of our power and have to face our powerlessness. However far removed we may be from the experience of the black pastor and his congregation, we all can recall similar moments in our own lives when we had at least a fleeting experience of the powerlessness that poor people suffer daily. Few of us would disagree that a condition of complete powerlessness, especially when it is socially imposed, is degrading and destructive.

As these stories of a dying woman and a struggling black pastor show, the experience of both power and weakness is etched into every human life. To be human is to exercise power, to seek to realize our possibilities, to help shape the world. At the same time, to be human is also to experience weakness, to become aware of dependence on persons and powers beyond ourselves. No one is absolutely independent. All of us live in a network of relationships with others. Human beings are social beings. We strive to become our own selves, but we can do so only as we continually receive the acceptance and help of others.

Let us probe a little more deeply this common human experience in which the question of God has its roots. Possessing power and experiencing powerlessness are as familiar as breathing in and out. Every human being, indeed every living creature, possesses and exercises power to some degree. There is no life where there is no power. Power is the ability to do something. It is the capacity to accomplish a purpose. We exercise power in every action, even in the smallest step we take. Yet as we act, we discover that we are not alone; we are surrounded by other powers. These other powers continually work upon us and make us more or less dependent. Thus we experience the reality of power both actively and passively. This is true of our personal development, of our social and political life, and of our dealings with the world of nature.

In every stage of development, human life is characterized by the power to be, to act, to create, to make a difference. An infant cries in order to get his mother's attention. This is, to be sure, a very small display of human power. But if the infant were unable to exercise even this seemingly insignificant power, he might be neglected and quite possibly die. The teenager affirms her independence from her parents. If she were to offer no resistance at all to her parents' ideas and expectations, her growth toward maturity and adulthood would be blocked. The need to share in the exercise of power is present in all stages of life. Life seeks power in the sense of new opportunities for development and self-expression.

We experience life as a field of interacting and often conflicting powers. Our exercise of power, from infancy onward, always meets some resistance. We exercise what power we have, and we are affected by the exercise of power by others. We are always both agents and patients, both centers and sufferers of power. Because of this, human development requires that we be able to trust in powers other than our own. According to developmental psychologists, a fundamental trust by the infant in the surrounding world, and especially in the mother, is an essential element in human growth. We cannot become mature, healthy persons without a basic trust in powers beyond our own. From infancy to old age we rely on one another. Human relationships are thus a delicate interplay of power exercised and power suffered. Sometimes we experience cooperation, partnership, and a sharing of power with others. More often we feel helpless and victimized by the power of others. On occasion we may even come to recognize that our own use of power has rendered others helpless.

We experience the interplay of power and powerlessness not only in our personal development but in our social, economic, and political life as well. As members of groups, companies, classes, and nations, we collectively exercise vast power. The power of one group is countered and challenged by the power of other groups. In international relations people speak of a balance or an imbalance of power. Indeed, the term "power" is most frequently used in this sociological and political meaning of the ability of one group or class or nation to have its way and to control others. As long as individuals share in the power exercised by an institution or a social order, they consider themselves powerful and free. Those who are excluded from the decision-making that affects their lives and are pushed to the margins of society experience powerlessness and bondage. They may resign themselves to their condition, or they may lash out in violence against a society that engages in crude or subtle institutionalized violence on them.

Finally, our dealings with nature also involve both the exercise of power and the experience of powerlessness. Through science and technology human beings have the ability to control many forces of nature and to use them for the achievement of human aims. The consequences of this exercise of power over nature are both good and evil. Modern industrial societies not only use but abuse the natural environment. Our declining energy resources and our polluted air, water, and fields show how far we have gone in making nature a victim of our exercise of power. On the other hand, human beings can still find themselves helpless before the awesome manifestations of natural power in hurricanes, earthquakes, volcanic eruptions, flood, and drought. We can also experience powerlessness to reverse the harmful effects that our abuse of nature has caused. Thus in our relationship with nature we are clearly both agents and sufferers of power.

Being human, then, has very much to do with the way power is exercised and the way powerlessness is suffered. Human beings need to possess some power, but they also need to be able to trust in the helpful exercise of power by others. We need power in order to be human, in order to live, to grow, to create, to give shape to our own life, and to help shape the world around us. At the same time, when power is used oppressively rather than cooperatively, it brings ruin and misery to all dimensions of life. Power can be used for good or evil. As the possibilities of exercising power for good increase, so also do the possibilities of exercising power for evil. It is hardly surprising that many people today are cynical about every form of power. With Lord Acton they say, "Power tends to corrupt and absolute power corrupts absolutely." There is truth in this statement, but it is not the whole truth. Powerlessness also tends to corrupt, and total powerlessness is a deadly threat to human life. We can lose our humanity by abusing power; we can also lose our humanity by supinely acquiescing in our powerlessness.

It is in the midst of real life where we exercise power and experience powerlessness that we raise the question about God. We may ask about God when we yearn to be forgiven of some guilt that threatens to paralyze us and rob us of all joy. We may ask about God when we experience the gradual or sudden loss of our power because of illness or old age. We may ask about God when we see innocent people tortured or killed by ruthless regimes. We may ask about God when we seek power to change oppressive conditions and to build a better world.

The urgency of the question of God is ignored in ivory tower debates about the existence of God or in cocktail party chatter about the latest theological fad. It arises in relation to the experience of the corruption of power and the experience of the abyss of powerlessness. Is there a power that does not crush human beings but empowers them and enters into creative partnership with them? Is there a power that does not oppress others but sets them free? Is there a power that does not deceive but can be trusted in life and in death? Is the ultimate power at work in this power-filled world friendly or hostile, gracious or malevolent, concerned or indifferent to our longing for transformed life? These are the real questions we ask when we ask about—God.

Faith in God as Reliance on the Ultimate Power

The question of God arises in response to our day-to-day experiences of power and powerlessness. In its deepest form the question of God is the question of the nature of ultimate power.

The close association of power and God is a universal religious phenomenon. In all religions God is experienced as awesome power, power that evokes wonder and fear. God is mysterious power that both attracts and repels us. The power of God is superior to all other powers because it has the capacity to create and to destroy. From the dawn of human history God has been the name of overwhelming power. The sages of ancient Greece taught that "all things are full of gods." Each of the gods of ancient Greek religion was connected with a life power experienced as irresistible or overwhelming: Aphrodite represented the power of sexual attraction; Dionysius, the power of wine and ecstatic joy; Athena, the power of wisdom; Apollo, the power of the arts; Ares, the power of war; Zeus, the power of destiny.

Although today we no longer give personal names to the powers that surround us, they are factors of life and compete for our allegiance. They compel us to ask which power we will acknowledge as ultimate. Faith in God involves a fundamental decision about the ultimate power at work in the world. In a recent study by George Gallup, Jr., entitled *The Search for America's Faith,* it is reported that 94 percent of American adults confess a belief in God or in a universal spirit. On the surface this is an impressive statistic. But in fact the question of whether God exists fails to get to the real issue of faith. The more telling questions to raise are: Who or what is the God in whom we trust? What do we believe God is really like? What difference does belief in God make in our everyday lives?

Our view of faith is superficial if we imagine that it involves no more than saying yes to the question: Does God exist? Authentic faith in God is something much deeper. Faith in God is confidence in the power that has created and rules the world. It is trust in the power that governs our lives and guides the course of history. It is commitment to the power that rightfully claims our worship and unconditional allegiance. It is reliance on the power worthy to judge us and able to save us.

Our real God is the power that we recognize, not just in theory but in everyday practice, as ultimate in our personal lives and in the whole world. Whatever we look to as the ultimate source of meaning and power in life is our God. Martin Luther expresses this point with great clarity. In a famous passage of his *Large Catechism* he writes: "A God is that to which we look for all good and where we resort for help in every time of need; to have a God is simply to trust and believe in one with our whole heart.... The confidence and faith of the heart alone make both God and an idol.... Whatever your heart clings to and confides in, that is really your God."

Luther's classic statement of what it means to believe in God says several things of great importance. In the first place, it brings out the fact that faith in God represents a passionate trust rather than mere intellectual curiosity or casual assent to traditional beliefs. A God is someone or something to which one looks for saving power, for wholeness and meaning in life, for "all good," for "help in every time of need." Faith in God is never partial; it involves the

whole person. In faith we entrust ourselves to God unconditionally, or as Luther says, with "our whole heart." Faith
means clinging to God in life and in death. It is affirming
that this power we call God judges and redeems us. It is
trusting that the one we call God is able to bring us and all
creatures to fulfillment and is thus the ultimate power at
work in this world. The passionate act of faith is far from
intellectual sport; it is a matter of life and death. Luther's
own religious quest went far beyond simply asking: Does
God exist? His burning question was: How can I find a
gracious, a benevolent, a saving God?

Secondly, Luther's statement implies that we may in fact
have a god even when we do not recognize this to be the
case. On the theoretical level, we may ignore or deny the
reality of God. But in actual life practice, we demonstrate
otherwise. However enlightened, agnostic, or even atheistic we may be in relation to traditional beliefs about God,
we nevertheless have a god. We recognize in practice one
of the powers within us or outside us as ultimate. We all
have our "ultimate concern" (Paul Tillich). We all give our
hearts to something, allow something to function—at least
for the time being—as our highest value, our highest
priority in life. We may not consciously acknowledge that it
is our ultimate concern—our god—but the fact is evident
from our practical decisions and our way of life.

In one of her short stories, Flannery O'Connor describes
a social worker named Sheppard. He is an enlightened man
who thinks that talk of demonic power and the need for the
redeeming power of Jesus is "rubbish." Sheppard is totally
dedicated to rescuing the underprivileged; it is his religion,
his ultimate concern. He is convinced that he is able,
through his own powers of intelligence, understanding, and
patience, to bring about the moral transformation of a mean
and hardened boy named Rufus. Consumed by his passion
to change Rufus, Sheppard neglects and even cruelly be-
rates his own son, who is only an average ten-year-old and

certainly far less intelligent than Rufus. In the end, Sheppard awakes to the fact that he has failed miserably in his effort to "save" Rufus and discovers, too late, that he has deprived his own son of the love that he needed.

Some of the ultimate concerns to which people wholeheartedly give themselves are noble and admirable, such as the cause of universal human rights and "liberty and justice for all"; other ultimate concerns are mean and shoddy, such as the pursuit of wealth, success, or endless sexual adventures; still other ultimate concerns are obviously demonic, such as militaristic nationalism or the spirit of racial superiority.

Whether we acknowledge it or not, we all recognize some cause, some principle, some power as ultimate in our life. Consciously or not, we entrust ourselves to this power perceived and valued as ultimate. In our hearts we confess, "Thou art my god." Of course, we may flit from one god to another. In our estrangement from the true God we are likely to have many gods. In any case, for as long as we have a particular god, we look to it as our ultimate power, and we rely on it for help in our helplessness.

Faith in God vs. Faith in the Gods

Luther's statement lights up still another feature of faith in God—the necessity of distinguishing between the true God and idols. Only God is worthy to be the object of our total and unconditional love and loyalty. The true God is radically different from the gods to whom we are tempted again and again to give our hearts. We may and do have many commitments; we may and do recognize the importance of many causes. If we have faith in God, however, we will refuse to allow any of these other concerns to become what is ultimately important in our life.

The God of the biblical witness is a "jealous" God. The first of the Ten Commandments declares emphatically:

"You shall have no other gods before me" (Ex. 20:3). God wants our complete and undivided trust and allegiance. When Jesus is asked what is the greatest of the commandments, he replies: "You shall love the Lord your God with all your heart, and with all your soul, and with all your mind" (Matt. 22:37). If we rightly understand and obey this commandment, we know why it is inseparably bound to another commandment: "You shall love your neighbor as yourself" (Matt. 22:39).

Love for one's family is a fine thing. But when it substitutes for love of God and love of all God's children, it becomes an idol.

Patriotism—the affection and loyalty one has for one's native land—is surely a noble sentiment. But when patriotism challenges or even replaces one's love for and loyalty to God and God's righteousness, it turns into an idol.

An idol is anything we substitute for the true God. We expect our idols to fill our lives with meaning, to make us happy, to supply us with whatever we need. We look to the idols to protect us from our doubts about our worth, from our feelings of guilt and emptiness, from our fears of weakness, suffering, and death. But the idols cannot deliver what we demand of them. Entrusting ourselves to idols leads not to fulfillment but to self-destruction and quite frequently to the destruction of others as well. Every idol is like the sorcerer in the legend of the Sorcerer's Apprentice. The power given to us by the idol quickly overpowers us and makes us its slave.

The idols of power are within us and around us. They compete for our allegiance. Knowledge is power, we are told. Money is power, others say. Power comes from the barrel of a gun, according to a revolutionary saying. These are only a few of the more common confessions of where ultimate power is sought and found in our time. The true God also exercises power. As the apostle Paul writes, "The kingdom of God does not consist in talk but in power" (I

Cor. 4:20). But the power of the Kingdom of God is different
from the power of the idols. Christ is "the power of God" (I
Cor. 1:24); the gospel is "the power of God for salvation"
(Rom. 1:16). When one entrusts oneself to the true God
whose power is radically different from all other powers,
one is thrust into the struggle between God and the gods.
Where faith in the God of the gospel dawns in human life,
the twilight of all our powerful gods begins.

During the late 1960s and early 1970s a movement called
"death of God" theology attracted national attention. It
proved to be a passing fad. It was influenced too much by
the optimistic spirit of the time. It judged that modern
science and technology made faith in God unnecessary.
This was a serious mistake. Today we are more aware that
the use of power in the modern world is thoroughly
ambiguous; it is both bane and blessing. If those who
occupy positions of power no longer ask the question of
God, certainly those who are the victims of a power-
dominated world continue to ask the question. Nevertheless, as a diagnosis of our social and cultural attitudes, there
was a measure of truth in the talk of the "death of God." We
experience and acknowledge powerfulness in the Pentagon
and the Kremlin, in nuclear weapons and laser beams, in
the huge oil companies and in OPEC, in technology and
gross national product, in the mass media and the super-
stars of popular culture. What can the power of the Kingdom of God mean in comparison with these very real and
awesome powers that control our lives?

If old gods die, new gods are born. Our age is far from
godless. The religion of modern people is polytheism—the
worship of many gods. Finite powers and limited causes are
elevated to divinity. The consumption of material goods
and reliance on nuclear armaments are among the many
gods that promise us fulfillment and claim our total allegiance. Advertisements ask us to believe that if we have
new cars, bigger homes, better clothes, and all sorts of

electronic gadgetry, we will find happiness. We are also encouraged to trust in more sophisticated and more powerful nuclear arms as a guarantee of our personal and national safety.

In view of the many gods that inhabit our world, we do well to recognize that the word "God" is much more ambiguous than is commonly thought. It has many different and even contradictory meanings. It is a word used to express love, and a word used to express hate. It is a word of blessing and a word of cursing. In the name of God the most selfless acts are performed, and in the name of God the most savage crusades have been undertaken. The word "God" seems to be able to stand for everything, and thus for nothing.

This is why faith in God—the living God of the Bible—must be distinguished continually from faith in the gods. The community of faith called the Christian church speaks of God not in general terms but according to the biblical witness to God who speaks and acts in particular ways. So defined, the word "God" is an inescapably controversial word. Faith in God draws us into a field of struggle and conflict. If we place our trust in God, we are driven into a struggle against other gods, both in our personal lives and in our wider social and political life. In this great struggle, faith in God always undermines commitment to other gods, and demotes them from the status of gods to that of finite powers placed under human responsibility.

We cannot think or speak properly of God, as the Bible uses this word, without taking part in this conflict between faith in God and faith in the gods. A choice must be made. A decision must be reached. As Elijah warned the people of Israel on Mt. Carmel, it is impossible to go limping forever back and forth between God and the gods (I Kings 18:20–21). The power of God is different from the power of the idols, and we are confronted with the choice as to which power we shall worship and serve. The prophets of the Old

Testament mock the gods made by human hands. These idols are lifeless. They cannot speak. They cannot act. They cannot even move. They have to be carried around by their makers (Isa. 46:5–7). The prophets repeatedly call the people to decide whether they will worship the living God or give themselves to idols whose promise of power appeals to self-centered interests.

Thus all our questions about God are like boomerangs. They have a way of turning back upon us and changing into the question: Who is the God whom *you* will trust in and serve?

As we shall try to show in the following chapters, the living God of the Bible is totally different from the idols that constantly claim our minds and affections. Although the Christian church and its theology have not always understood this fact, God's power is radically different from the power exercised by our personal or corporate idols. The true God searches for us long before we begin to search for God. The true God is majestically strong, yet shows that strength most awesomely in humility and weakness. The true God is not the guarantor of the way things are but the disturbing God who keeps us restless for a new world. The true God is not oppressive but liberating. The true God is not a reflection of ourselves and our society but a surprising God who continually challenges all our presuppositions about what it means to be human and what it means to be divine. God is altogether unlike the dead idols which we fabricate with our hands or construct in our imaginations. The true God is the God strong enough to live with and for others. This God is not the enemy but the friend of humanity. Love of this different God must be inseparably united with love of our neighbor and respect for the worth of all creatures.

The difference between God and the gods, between saving power and pseudo power, is crucial to a proper understanding of faith in God. So it was in the time of the prophets of ancient Israel; so it was in the time of Jesus of Nazareth; so it is in our own time, in which power is exercised by many so destructively and suffered by many more so grievously.

2
IMAGES OF GOD'S POWER IN MODERN SOCIETY

Knowledge of God and Knowledge of Ourselves

At the beginning of his *Institutes of the Christian Religion*, John Calvin declares that knowledge of God and knowledge of ourselves are deeply intertwined. We never have one without the other. As Calvin explains, if we begin with self-knowledge and admit how weak and needy we are, immediately we are led to consider how great and majestic God is. On the other hand, if we begin with a confession of the beauty and holiness of God, we are prompted at once to acknowledge our own unhappiness and sinfulness. Our images of God and our images of ourselves develop together.

Calvin's principle of the interplay of knowledge of God and knowledge of ourselves operates in the life of every believer and in the worship and witness of the community of faith. We think and speak of God in metaphors and images drawn from human experience. No idea or image of God drops straight down from heaven. Our thinking and speaking of God are conditioned by human experience and shaped by human imagination.

Consider the rich variety of images which the Bible employs in speaking of God. Some of these images are taken from the world of nature—God is like a rock (Ps. 28:1), a light (Ps. 27:1), a fire (Ex. 3:2). Other images come from the sphere of personal relationships—God is like a mother (Isa. 49:14–15), a father (Matt. 7:11), a husband (Hos. 2:16), a friend (Jer. 3:4). Still others come from the world of work—God is like a shepherd (Ps. 23:1), a potter (Rom. 9:21), a builder of a city (Heb. 11:10). And still others come from the political sphere—God is like a king (I Sam. 12:12), a lord (Rev. 17:14), a judge (Isa. 33:22). All of this shows that our language about God is essentially metaphorical and involves the exercise of human imagination.

While cherishing the diversity of biblical images of God, the Christian community has always placed special emphasis on the more personal images. This emphasis has sometimes been criticized as "anthropomorphism," which means thinking and speaking as if God resembled a human being. Some philosophers and theologians would prefer to call God the Supreme Being, or Being-itself, or the First Cause, or the Highest Good. But such language seems cold and abstract to most believers. In any case, the Bible shows little hesitation in speaking of God with the help of "anthropomorphic" images. With vivid simplicity, it speaks of the strong arm of God, or of God's having compassion on the poor or being outraged by injustice. Despite obvious dangers, speaking of God in personal terms has always seemed appropriate to Christians in every age for two basic reasons. First, we are created in the "image of God" (Gen. 1:27), which symbolizes not physical likeness but a similarity of life in personal relationship. And second, in the incarnation God has freely entered human life and thus authorized personal images of God. For Christians the person Jesus of Nazareth is the perfect "image of the invisible God" (Col. 1:15). He is the "human face of God" (J. A. T. Robinson).

It is, however, one thing to speak of ourselves as created in God's image and to confess that Jesus Christ is the decisive and complete image of God. It is something entirely different to think and speak of God as made in *our* image, to describe the reality of God as simply a bigger and

stronger version of ourselves, to understand God's power as
the magnification of whatever power enlarges us. This way
leads to idolatry. We then imagine God so as to suit our own
wants and interests. We project ourselves onto the reality
we call God. The human imagination is extraordinarily
skilled in making God look, think, and act just like us. In its
captivity to sin, our imagination works like "a perpetual
factory of idols," to use Calvin's words. We think of God as
a mirror image of our sinful selves; God confirms our ideals,
endorses our priorities and values, upholds and defends our
way of life.

Calvin's criticism of making God in our own image
applies to both church and society today. All of our knowledge of God, like other kinds of knowledge, is colored by
personal and group interests. Our personal interests are
often obvious to us and to others. More subtle, however, are
the ways in which our thinking and acting are influenced
by the economic and social interests of the communities to
which we belong. If we are beneficiaries of the present
social order, we are likely to insist upon its being upheld
and defended. On the other hand, if we experience oppression or severe disadvantage in the present social order, we
are likely to have a strong interest in promoting changes
that will improve our lot and that of others in our condition.
These conflicting human interests will affect our thinking
and speaking about God. Moses believed that God wanted
the Hebrew slaves in Egypt to go free. Pharaoh clearly
thought otherwise. Our knowledge of God—and in particular our understanding of divine power—is influenced by
our prevailing economic and social interests. Theology that
fails to take this fact into account is neither serious nor
honest. To paraphrase Calvin, our self-centered, class-
centered, and nation-centered interests are a perpetual
source of idols.

The movement between knowledge of God and knowledge of ourselves goes both ways. If it is true that we shape

our understanding of God in terms of what we consider valuable and desirable, it is also true that we try to model ourselves after whatever we imagine God to be like. We develop our humanity according to the image of the God who rules our life. If our god is a warrior bent on conquest, we will gladly march off to annihilate our enemies. If our god is a merciless judge of all who transgress the established law, we will be similarly severe and judgmental of all transgressors.

The interplay of distorted images of self and distorted images of God is vividly portrayed by Sherwood Anderson in his story of Jesse Bentley in *Winesburg, Ohio.* A pious, prosperous, and hardworking farmer, Jesse comes from a long line of strong men. He wants his farm to produce more than any other farm in the state. Above all, he wants to be the father of sons who will be rulers, just as the biblical Jesse was.

Jesse believes in an austere and powerful God who controls human destiny but who remains hidden. He believes he is following God's will by working hard to acquire possessions, by exercising dominion over the earth, by ruling over the members of his family and others dependent on him, and by siring male children who will be rulers in their turn.

As he grows older and more prosperous, Jesse is no longer content with his six hundred acres. He covets his neighbor's property as well. Convinced he is God's chosen, Jesse looks upon his neighbors as Philistines, enemies of God. He fears that a Goliath will come from these Philistines to take away his land and possessions. So Jesse prays for a son whom he will call David. Eventually a grandson by that name comes under his charge. One day the grandfather accompanies the young boy into the forest. The boy intends to go hunting with his slingshot, but Jesse secretly plans to sacrifice a lamb and dedicate his grandson to God. Frightened by his grandfather's strange behavior, David

runs away. When Jesse pursues him, the terrified boy picks
up a stone, places it in his slingshot and hurls it at the old
man. Jesse is stunned and rendered helpless; the boy is
never seen again.

The symbolism of this story is as profound as it is familiar.
In his lust for power, Jesse fears the coming of a Goliath
who will take away his land. Yet Jesse himself has become
an oppressive Goliath whose destructive dream of power is
finally ended by the slingshot of a frightened young boy.
Jesse's hunger for power costs him his beloved grandson.
His understanding of power, divine and human, is his
undoing. As in the biblical story, the power of God proves
to be at work not in strong Goliath but in weak David.

Anderson's story helps us to grasp how knowledge of God
and knowledge of ourselves interlock. It also helps us to see
what is at stake in the choice between the power of God and
the power of idols conceived after our own image. Religion
is by no means always a safe and beneficial activity. What
we imagine God to be like profoundly affects human life for
good or for evil. Faith in the living God is a humanizing
force; faith in idols molded by our egocentrism and ethno-
centrism is a terribly destructive force. There can be no
knowledge of God apart from the work of human imagination, but our imagination must be liberated from the chains
of self-interests and parochial group interests that bind it.

Distorted Images of Divine Power

In order to examine further the reciprocal relationship
between our images of God and our self-images, let us look
at three prominent images of God in modern society. These
images are not often expressed openly, and this list does not
exhaust the ways in which God's power is understood by
people today. But the following images of God are present
and influential in modern society and unfortunately all too
often in the church as well. Human interests and fears are

clearly reflected in these images of God.

1. For many people today, both inside and outside the church, God is imagined as the *supreme monarch.* The power of God the monarch is coercive power, the power of brute force and compulsion. God's power is here equated with arbitrary and totalitarian force. It is sheer almightiness, unqualified omnipotence. The authority that God has over us is based on absolute and unlimited power. God is like earthly monarchs who do whatever they please. As the philosopher Charles Hartshorne suggests, some people may have a boss at work who rules like a dictator and they may be inclined to think of God as the "world boss" who is in complete control of everything. The God who is supreme monarch or world boss must not be questioned. And since the hierarchy of the church is supposed to speak for God, what the hierarchy says is the last word. If we raise questions, we are simply told: "This has always been the teaching of the church. It must be believed and obeyed. No dissent or doubt will be tolerated." So by analogy with God's imperial power, the power of the church in declaring what must be believed and practiced is absolutized. It is said to be free from all error and never in need of correction.

According to some theologians, this idea of divine almightiness is enshrined in the traditional image of God as "Father." God is the great patriarch, lording it over the lesser members of the family or tribe. God the Father, so it is charged, is the archetype of the domineering male who demands that others submit unconditionally to his will. While some persons may find this charge farfetched, there is little reason to doubt that the father image has become a problem for a number of men and women today. It is often an image to be rebelled against rather than the symbol of a reality to be respected and loved. The father image, it is claimed, is not just the image of sexist oppression but the image of authoritarian power in all spheres of life—in education, church, business, and politics. In all these areas, the "fathers" possess and exercise coercive power.

This view of God's power—as the controlling power of the supreme monarch, world boss, or domineering father—sets belief in God in irreconcilable conflict with all the movements of enlightenment and emancipation that have characterized modern society. God becomes the symbol of repression and resistance to change. For some men and women today the question of God's power has become the question of whether there is an ultimate power different from—wholly other than—the power of control and compulsion so familiar in our personal and social histories and often symbolically associated with the figure of the authoritarian father.

If the church continues to employ the image of God as Father (which it should), the image must certainly be rid of its patriarchal connotations. If the church continues to employ the image of God as Lord (which it should), the image must be clearly distinguished from dictatorship and bossism.

2. According to a second view, God is understood as a *captive power*, a power under our control. This view of God takes many forms. In one form, God is understood as a kind of business partner. We are related to God by an exchange process; there is a trade-off between God and us. This is expressed in religion that is based on a system of merit. We are repaid for our good deeds or for our performances of ritual. This repayment may come in the form of happiness and success in the present; or it may be postponed to another life after death. In any case, God is imagined as having entered into a contractual relationship with us that is based essentially on the principle of merit or business exchange. There is thus a happy correspondence between our relationship with God and the underlying principles of our economic and social systems.

The captive God also appears under the guise of a

fabulous magician who is asked to pull all sorts of rabbits out of the hat for our benefit. If you want a promotion at work or a new car or a winning ticket in the lottery, just ask the great magician and you will have your wish.

The essence of every image of the captive God is that we are able to manipulate the divine. All power is viewed as manipulable, and God happens to be the manipulable power of supreme interest to us. The practice of trying to manipulate God is very old. It is called magic. According to magical religion, divine power can be harnessed by the proper ritual or the right words to bring about a desired effect. While we may dismiss this view of God as a feature of archaic religions, there are many ways in which believers today try to manipulate God for their own interests. The more repulsive forms of manipulation of God or of belief in God are found in a fictional figure like Elmer Gantry—a successful con artist in the form of a revivalist preacher—or in a real-life figure like Jim Jones of Jonestown, Guyana, whose manipulative techniques led finally to mass suicide. But the self-interested use of God is a much more common practice than these universally repudiated figures suggest. The name of God is "used" when it is made the religious foundation of a nationalistic fervor, or of a political movement, or of a particular economic system or way of life. God is used by the television preacher who promises healing for an infirmity if the viewer will only say a little prayer or place her afflicted limb against the television screen or send in a cash contribution.

In these and many other ways, God is taken captive by us. God is compelled to serve our personal wishes or our social and economic interests or projects. Our captive God is given our allegiance to the extent that we get what we want, to the extent that we are made happy now or in the hereafter, to the extent that we are shown that God is on our side and upholds the values we espouse. Such a God is useful to us in establishing and maintaining what we

consider to be the good and happy life. The captive God is
our supreme genie, our personal or national champion.

The modern criticism of religion draws much of its
strength from these closely related images of God as business partner, magician, and champion—all views of God as
a captive, manipulable deity, who serves our infantile
demands and who sometimes enters into an unholy alliance
with misery and injustice. The images of God as manipulable power create bad faith. Such views of God are severely
criticized by Marxists, and their criticism surely contains
some measure of truth. But the critique of the manipulable
God has a source far deeper and stronger than Marxism.
The prophets of Israel and Jesus of Nazareth struggled
against the manipulable God long before Marx. They pro-
claimed the living God who is altogether different from the
little gods manufactured by our fears and desires. The
living God shatters our distorted images of divinity and
stands in judgment on every effort to manipulate divine
power and grace.

3. A third image of God in modern society is that of *pure
transcendence:* God exists in isolation from the world.
According to this view, God is the absolute, perfect, and
unconditioned reality. Absolute means totally unrelated to
anything else. The power of God is imagined as above and
outside, unconnected with worldly events and human history. God is entirely free from the suffering and misery of
the world. God is, strictly speaking, indifferent and apathetic. This is an image of God with a long history. Aristotle
spoke of God as the "Unmoved Mover," the supreme being
who moves the world by the power of attraction but
remains entirely unmoved and unaffected by what happens
in the world. Eternity is untouched by time. God is alone in
splendid perfection, not wanting or needing anything. God
has no friends, said Aristotle, because to have a friend is to
be affected by another. The ancient Stoics also imagined
the supreme reality as indifferent and apathetic and tried to

adopt that detached attitude as much as possible in their own life. Through apathy one becomes invulnerable to the affliction of this world.

In the eighteenth century a modified version of this image of God appeared in a form called deism. According to the deists, God created the world and then allowed it to run entirely on its own. God is too great and too exalted to be intimately involved with the day-to-day affairs of the world. Like an expert clockmaker, God has made the world to run completely on its own. The more clockmakers have to repair their clocks, the less mastery they display. God is the perfect clockmaker whose supreme ability is expressed in the world process, which needs no divine assistance. The God of deism is an armchair deity.

In our time the doctrine of the indifference and aloofness of God has many sources and assumes many different forms. One source is modern individualism. The ideal or strong individual is supposed to be totally independent of others. Many popular self-help philosophies, which talk a lot about self-realization, presuppose this understanding of human selfhood. Each individual possesses all necessary value and power within the self. The self must contend and negotiate with other selves, but relationship with others is not really essential. The image of an absolute, indifferent god goes hand in hand with the image of the individual human being as an absolutely independent self.

The image of the absolute god and the corresponding image of the solitary self are socially and spiritually bankrupt. We are becoming increasingly aware today of the interdependence of all life. The idea of an absolutely independent, completely self-made individual is a destructive myth. If it is an error to idealize the utterly self-sufficient human being, it is equally mistaken and equally destructive to think and speak of God as absolute and aloof. The image of God as absolute may be philosophically sophisticated, but it holds little comfort for people whose lives are crushed by unrelieved suffering or unforgiven guilt. The murder of millions of Jews in Nazi Germany and the massacre of millions in Stalin's concentration camps would mean nothing to the Unmoved Mover. The loss of a child in an absurd automobile accident would have no effect on the indifferent God. The affliction suffered by a cancer patient would meet with no response from the god who is defined as absolute, transcendent perfection.

There is, of course, the very real experience of the absence and silence of God. Job experienced this terrible absence. The human experience of the absence of God was most acutely felt by Jesus on the cross when he cried out: "My God, my God, why hast thou forsaken me?" (Mark 15:34). But the experience of the absence and silence of God is something entirely different from the view of God as uninterested and unrelated to us. The passion of Jesus' cry and the fact that in utmost affliction he dared to protest to God show that his fundamental relationship to God was altogether different from what would be possible with an apathetic deity. We can hardly overemphasize the point that the modern image of the isolated, indifferent god is an idol that reflects more our modern individualism than the reality of the living God.

The Partial Truth of Atheism

The images of the tyrannical god, the captive god, and the apathetic god are grotesque distortions of the Christian understanding of the ultimate power we call God. What is at stake in these distortions is not simply a mistaken doctrine of God. As we have seen, our images of God and our understandings of self and society influence each other. The issue is not one of theory only but also of practice. Where there is distortion in our understanding of God, there is also distortion in our understanding and practice of human life. When we misconceive divine power, we are also prone to misconceive and misuse human power.

The image of the domineering God breeds fear, resentment, and rebellion. If God's rule over us takes the form of unlimited control over impotent subjects, then the master-slave relationship in human society finds justification in religious belief. The only way to be free from coercive power exercised by the omnipotent god and earthly tyrants is to repudiate their authority and actually or symbolically to destroy them.

The image of the captive God breeds complacency, self-deception, and exploitation. If God can be bought off, if God can be used to satisfy our every whim and desire, why should not fellow creatures also be so used? Moreover, if God is on our side, then we must always be in the right, and whatever we do to further our cause will have God's blessing. The captive God is unable to exercise judgment on us and unable to act in new and unexpected ways. Our self-interests and our established way of life become the measure of all things, including God.

The image of the indifferent God breeds hopelessness and resignation. If God is aloof and unaffected by what happens in the world, then the beauty and tragedy, the joy and affliction of life have no real and lasting significance. What happens in time is "a tale told by an idiot, full of sound and fury, signifying nothing." Depression and despair seem the only option for suffering and oppressed men and women if the ultimate power that rules the universe is unaffected by their cries.

Thus Christian faith in God acknowledges the partial truth of atheistic critiques of religion. All of our understandings and images of God must undergo a testing of the most radical sort. Even the biblical images of God, such as "Father" and "Lord," are not immune to this process of critical testing. The process begins with our accustomed and unexamined understanding of a symbol for God such as "father." That symbol must then undergo testing and criticism. We gradually become aware that the Bible employs many different images of God, including those of father *and* mother. We also learn that when Jesus calls God "father," he does not mean the authoritarian and oppressive father figure so familiar to many people from history or from personal experience. Jesus redefines the meaning of God as father. Only when we have permitted the symbol of father to go through the fire of critical testing and have retrieved its fundamental biblical meaning are we able to use it again freely and gladly.

Jürgen Moltmann, a prominent contemporary theologian, has written the following proposition about the partial truth of atheism: "Only an atheist can be a good Christian; only a Christian can be a good atheist." This is a highly paradoxical statement. It requires careful interpretation, for on the surface it appears to be sheer nonsense.

The first half of the paradox—"Only an atheist can be a good Christian"—should be understood to mean that it is necessary to expose our idols as false gods in order to clarify Christian faith in God. Faith in God struggles against faith in the gods. There is no genuine faith without this struggle. There is no faith in the true God without also disbelieving in—saying a mighty "No" to—the gods who reflect our own narrow wishes and the exclusive interests of our society. In this sense there is a long tradition of "atheism" in Christianity. During the first few centuries of the church, Christians were charged with atheism because they refused to acknowledge and worship the gods of the Roman state. Thus a Christian need not be afraid of the critique of the gods by unbelievers. Indeed, much of their criticism may be true. It can even serve to purify authentic faith in God. To pretend that ideas of God do not sometimes function as infantile dreams of omnipotence (Freud) or as a kind of drug that anesthetizes people to the wretchedness and suffering of life (Marx) is to stick one's head in the sand like an ostrich. Faith in the living God puts the gods of our making to flight. There is a place for atheism in Christian faith and life in the sense that what is denied is not the reality of the living God but false and dehumanizing conceptions of God. Believing in God is impossible for some people not because they reject the reality of God but because they cannot accept woefully inadequate conceptions of God.

The second half of Moltmann's paradox is equally important: "Only a Christian can be a good atheist." That is to say, only faith in the living God is able to protect and promote what the atheist holds to be of great value—our true humanity. The atheist denies God for the sake of humanity, for a world free of injustice and oppression in which men and women can hold their heads high. The God of Christian faith, however, is not the enemy but the friend of true human freedom. Thus when atheists in their justified repudiation of the idols reject also the true God of the biblical witness, they open the door to the rule of human life by new idols. When they have cast out one demon, many more enter in unobserved (cf. Luke 11:24–26). After the disclosure of the horrors of the labor camps and the systematic repression of dissidents in officially atheistic societies, it is no longer possible to pretend that atheism automatically brings increased concern for human freedom and welfare and the unimpeded pursuit of truth.

In every age faith in God must contend with the gods of human imagination that control our personal lives and our social existence. The God of the biblical witness is different. Our life becomes truly human when faith in God is boldly and continuously distinguished from faith in the gods of our own making—the gods of brute force, self-centeredness, and indifference. Paul Lehmann, an influential American theologian, has gathered into a single phrase the practical significance of faith in God. Christian faith in God, Lehmann insists, centers on the issue of "making and keeping human life human." This is simply the other side of letting and continuing to let God be God. Human life becomes and remains human when it is lived in trust and confidence in the God whose power is different from all other powers. The power of this God is the power of liberating and reconciling love.

3
THE BIBLICAL WITNESS
TO GOD'S POWER

The Transformation of Our Knowledge of God
by the Biblical Witness

People claim to have knowledge of God from many different sources. They may see traces of God in the beauty and
order of nature. "The heavens are telling the glory of God,"
the psalmist writes (Ps. 19:1); the created order bears
witness to God's power and deity, the apostle Paul contends (Rom. 1:18ff.). In addition to finding traces of God in
nature, individuals and communities may see the mighty
hand of God in various events. A special turning point in
one's personal life, a momentous event of national or world
history, an act of great heroism, the birth of a child, the loss
of a close friend—these are some of the many occasions in
which the presence and power of God may be seen.

The knowledge of God that comes from these common
experiences is dim and ambiguous at best. Some theologians go so far as to deny all knowledge of God that does not
come directly from God's revelation in Jesus Christ. But
this extreme view is untenable. There is no disputing the
fact that people have some ideas of God or the gods and
form images of divine power prior to and apart from their
encounter with the gospel message. The real issue is not
whether some sort of knowledge of God is available on the
basis of common experience, but how such knowledge is

related to the biblical witness.

As our earlier chapters showed, sin continually distorts our knowledge of God. Our images of God often serve our drive for power and enhance our personal and corporate interests. The truth of God is turned into a lie, and the creature is worshiped instead of the Creator (Rom. 1:25). Recognizing the chronic human tendency to distort the knowledge of God, the Westminster Confession states: "Although the light of nature and the works of creation and providence do so far manifest the goodness, wisdom, and power of God as to leave men inexcusable, yet they are not sufficient to give that knowledge of God, and of his will, which is necessary unto salvation."

All of the great world religions speak of God on the basis of a particular tradition. Their knowledge of God is not vague and general but historically definite and concrete. It is mediated through the life and worship of a particular community of faith, through particular scriptures, through the telling and retelling of a particular story of a decisive revelation of God. The Christian understanding of God rests upon that special revelation of God's activity to which the Bible bears unique witness.

Christians look to the Bible for special illumination of the reality called God and the nature of the power God exercises. Throughout the history of the church, the Bible has shaped Christian life and the Christian imagination. This is not because Christians reverence the Bible as a book that has fallen down from heaven. The significance of the Bible does not lie in some theory of its supernatural origin or in some doctrine of its total inerrancy. The Bible is not read correctly when it is treated as an encyclopedia of revealed truths. The Bible is more like an epic drama than an encyclopedia.

Christians look to the Bible primarily because it contains the story of God's creative and redemptive activity. The biblical story plays a normative role in the life of the

Christian community. It tells us who God is and who we are as sinful creatures addressed by the judgment and grace of God. By listening to and living with the stories, teachings, prayers, warnings, and promises of the Bible, we see God and ourselves in a new light. We see the world as it is and as God intends it to be. We could easily imagine a Christian community without church buildings or robed choirs or clergy with doctoral degrees. But we cannot imagine a Christian community that does not repeatedly listen and respond to the biblical story. The telling and retelling of the great drama of the Bible identifies the character of God for us and establishes our Christian identity. Our faith in God is nourished in an irreplaceable way by this source.

Still more specifically, the Christian community turns to the Bible because of its unique and authoritative witness to God's mighty acts which culminate in the person of Jesus Christ and in the sending of his Spirit. The Christian community understands the reality and purpose of God in the light of the crucified and risen Jesus. Although there is some knowledge of God apart from this revelation, for Christians at least, the norm and center of all knowledge of God, whatever its source, is the biblical story of the cruci-fied Lord. For Christian faith he is the definitive revelation of God and hence the decisive embodiment of the power of God. All understandings of divine power are judged and transformed by his life, ministry, death, and resurrection. A Christian knowledge of God's power is not limited to what Jesus says and does and suffers, but this is its center and standard.

Thus the biblical story with its climax in Jesus Christ challenges and often turns upside down our previous knowledge of God. Christians will readily agree that there are always countless ideas of God in circulation. They will refuse, however, to accept any of these ideas uncritically. The proclamation of the gospel draws all of our ideas and images of God into a continual process of correction and transformation. We are never finished with learning and relearning what it means to understand God in the light of the gospel rather than on the basis of the idols of our imagination.

Even our most cherished images and names of God have to be reformed and transformed. If we call God "love," the meaning of this symbol is not to be determined finally by what we think we know about love on the basis of our personal experience or our cultural assumptions. The love of God is defined in a radically new way by the gospel story. The same is true of the "freedom" of God. Just as God's love is not to be confused with sentimentality, so God's freedom is radically different from doing whatever one pleases. Similarly, the biblical understanding of the power of God does not merely echo what we say ultimate power must be like. The biblical witness is a "Copernican revolution" in all of our presumed understandings of the power of God and of authentic human power. A fundamental shift in our thinking occurs. Just as Copernicus revolutionized astronomy by declaring that the earth rotates around the sun rather than the sun around the earth, so Christians participate in a revolution in thinking about God's power by finding the center, not in our own ideas or assumptions about power, but in Jesus Christ.

The Exodus Power of God

From beginning to end the Bible proclaims the sovereign power of God. The Bible opens with the majestic declaration: "In the beginning God created the heavens and the earth" (Gen. 1:1). And it ends with jubilant affirmations of the coming triumph of God at the conclusion of history: "Hallelujah! For the Lord our God the Almighty reigns" (Rev. 19:6). In between these visions of the beginning and end of history the Bible proclaims the mighty deeds of God. The psalmist sings praises to God the Creator and Redeemer: "Great is our LORD, and abundant in power" (Ps. 147:5).

The Bible contains a chorus of voices rather than one solitary voice. Israel's faith in God developed over many centuries, and as a result there are many strands in the Old Testament tradition. We are presented not with a single image of God but with a rich diversity of images. Each contributes to a full understanding of the power of God according to the faith of Israel.

Israel shared many beliefs about God with its neighbors of the ancient Near East. Like them, Israel could associate God's power with the phenomena of storm, lightning, and thunder. Like them, Israel could speak of God's power in the awesome vitality of nature, in the fertility of plants, animals, and human beings. Israel, too, could praise the power of the warrior God and declare God's superiority in battle. But we would not yet grasp what is distinctive in Israel's faith in God by placing primary emphasis on these elements of the Old Testament tradition. One image of God deserves our special attention because of its extraordinary importance: The God of the Old Testamant is the exodus God.

The power of God is celebrated by Israel first and foremost in the story of God's surprising liberation of a poor and oppressed people. The core confession of the Old Testament—"The LORD brought us out of Egypt with a mighty hand" (Deut. 26:5–9)—narrates the exodus of the people of Israel from bondage in Egypt by the power of God. God is the exodus God. The power of God is the power to set the oppressed free. We cannot overstate the revolutionary novelty of this experience and description of God's power. Once and for all, the power of God is distinguished from oppressive, authoritarian power. God is the power that makes for human freedom in a world of bondage. This stunning redefinition of God appears not in the form of a philosophical discourse but in the form of historical narrative. "I am the LORD your God who brought

you out of the land of Egypt, out of the house of bondage"
(Ex. 20:2). God's power is liberating power. It is known
decisively in an event of political, social, and religious
liberation. The image of the exodus God shatters all ideas of
God as author and guarantor of oppressive rule.

While the image of God as exodus God is immensely
important, it does not stand alone in the Old Testament. It
is deepened and enriched by other images of God. The God
who liberates an oppressed people also establishes a cove-
nant with them. God promises to be faithful and in turn
calls the people to faithfulness. God gives to the people of
Israel the law that is to order their life and make justice and
peace a concrete reality. Thus the power of God is both
liberating and demanding, both a power that grants freedom to those in bondage and a power that makes for justice
on the earth. This two-sidedness of God's power—its gift of
freedom and its demand of justice which accompanies this
gift—is an unmistakable feature of the Old Testament
witness. The liberty that God wills for all creatures is not
anarchic or self-centered but is expressed in justice and
regard for others, especially the poor and the weak.

That God's power is justice-making power is central to
the message of the great prophets of Israel. "[Israel] judged
the cause of the poor and needy; then it was well. Is not this
to know me? says the LORD" (Jer. 22:16). "He has showed
you, O man, what is good; and what does the LORD require
of you but to do justice, and to love kindness, and to walk
humbly with your God?" (Micah 6:8). The liberating power
of God, the prophets warn, is abused and corrupted if it is
not seen as the foundation of justice in human life. To know
the exodus God—the God who sets prisoners free—is to do
justice.

The faith of Israel moves from this center outward. It
begins with the experience of God's powerfulness in the
event of liberation from bondage and in the justice claims of
the law. From this point it reaches out to embrace the

destiny of all nations and all of nature. Just as Israel owes its existence to God who created a nation out of a group of "nobodies" enslaved by a world empire, so all things and all peoples have come into being by the sheer grace of their creator. Through Israel God's promise extends to all people. The Book of Jonah teaches that God wants not only Israel but all nations to repent and experience new life. The creator of Israel is no provincial deity but the Lord of all nations and the creator of heaven and earth (Gen. 1:1ff.). God's liberating and justice-making power encompasses the whole world.

If God's liberating power includes the call to justice, it is also understood as compassionate power. The hallmark of the God of the Old Testament is steadfast love. Although still popular in some quarters, it is a complete distortion to contrast the God of the Old Testament as a God of raw power and unforgiving justice with the God of the New Testament as a God of tender love and infinite mercy. According to the Old Testament, God hears the cries of the oppressed, has compassion on them and acts for their liberation from bondage. God is sympathetic to the cause of people who are weak and easily abused—widows, orphans, strangers, the poor. It is because God shares the pain of these helpless people that justice is commanded.

God's compassionate power reaches out to people in their sin, in their forgetfulness of the freedom bestowed on them, in their violation of the justice demanded of them. Unlike other gods, the God of Israel shows power in the form of mercy and forgiveness. "Who is a God like thee, pardoning iniquity and passing over transgression for the remnant of his inheritance? He does not retain his anger for ever because he delights in steadfast love" (Micah 7:18). God's compassion is like that of a mother for her beloved children (Isa. 66:12ff.). The theme of the faithful parental love of God is beautifully expressed by the prophet Hosea:

When Israel was a child, I loved him,
  and out of Egypt I called my son.
The more I called them,
  the more they went from me;
They kept sacrificing to the Baals,
  and burning incense to idols.
Yet it was I who taught Ephraim to walk,
  I took them up in my arms;
    but they did not know that I healed them.
I led them with cords of compassion,
  with the bands of love,
And I became to them as one
  who eases the yoke on their jaws,
    and I bent down to them and fed them. . . .

How can I give you up, O Ephraim!
  How can I hand you over, O Israel!
How can I make you like Admah!
  How can I treat you like Zeboiim!
My heart recoils within me,
  my compassion grows warm and tender.
I will not execute my fierce anger,
  I will not again destroy Ephraim;
for I am God and not man,
  the Holy One in your midst,
  and I will not come to destroy.
                          (Hos. 11:1–4, 8–9)

In addition to the justice and compassion that are associated with God's liberating power, another important element of the Old Testament witness to the exodus God must be mentioned. The power of God is experienced both as a reality and as a promise. Liberation has come, and yet it needs to come again and in still greater depth and scope. Justice is sometimes experienced, but more often injustice, exploitation, and cruelty reign. The compassion of God is from time to time an experienced reality, but there is also the terrible experience of the absence and silence of God. The Old Testament knows joy but also lamentation and affliction. Israel thus yearns for the full realization of God's justice in all the earth. This yearning is unforgettably expressed in The Book of Job and in the cries of the psalmists and prophets. "O that thou wouldst rend the heavens and come down" (Isa. 64:1). The Old Testament proclaims the exodus God, and it looks forward with burning anticipation to a new and greater exodus.

The Power of the Crucified and Risen Christ

The New Testament is based on Israel's faith in God and God's lordship over all things. The God and Father of Jesus Christ is the God of Israel. Jesus does not proclaim a new God but the same God whose word was spoken by the prophets of Israel. Jesus announces the nearness of the one and only God who sends rain on the just and the unjust (Matt. 5:45) and who feeds the birds of the air and adorns the lilies of the field (Matt. 6:26ff.). What is new in the New Testament is not merely a new teaching about God. What is new is the personal presence of God in Jesus of Nazareth. The new thing is Jesus himself as the human image of God, the "living parable" of God (Edward Schillebeeckx). As the author of Hebrews says, "In many and various ways God spoke of old to our fathers by the prophets; but in these last days he has spoken to us by a Son" (Heb. 1:1–2a). In Jesus' action, passion, and resurrection Christians find the decisive revelation of the reality and power of God. If the key image of God in the Old Testament is the event of the exodus, the central image of God in the New Testament is a person, Jesus of Nazareth—what he does, what he suffers, what comes of his life. In her song at the annunciation of the birth of Jesus, Mary summarizes the new understanding of divine power which is expressed in the story of Jesus— God has "put down the mighty from their thrones, and exalted those of low degree" (Luke 1:52).

Jesus proclaims the coming of the reign of God in the power of the Spirit. Who God is and what the lordly rule of God is like are made known by Jesus both in the form of teaching and in the concrete language of action. Not only is Jesus' teaching characterized by astonishing authority (Mark 1:22), but he casts out evil powers from human life (Mark 1:27). He proclaims good news to the poor (Luke 6:20), and he announces the day of liberation to those in bondage (Luke 4:18f.). He dares to forgive sins. He has table fellowship with sinners and other despised people. He heals the sick and even raises the dead. In his healings and in his forgiveness of sins Jesus brings the transforming power of God into every corner of human life.

These liberating actions bring Jesus into collision with the religious and political leaders. Some scribes and Pharisees are outraged by Jesus and his claim to be inaugurating the long-awaited deliverance of God. Jesus proclaims and serves not a God of the social and religious status quo but a liberating God. He boldly calls God "Abba" ("dear father"), and teaches his disciples to pray to God as "our heavenly father." This expression of intimate relationship with God is a sign of the radically new understanding of God and of divine power that informs the life and ministry of Jesus. But what is even more disturbing to the opponents of Jesus is that he addresses God as "dear father" while engaging in liberating activity on behalf of sinners and the oppressed. The God Jesus calls father is not a God who oppresses but a God who loves and forgives so that people can be set free. What Jesus means by calling God father cannot be determined by ideas of fatherhood derived from sources outside the Gospel narrative. The meaning of God as father is defined by Jesus' struggle against those who have turned God into an instrument of legalistic oppression.

The disturbance caused by Jesus is evident in many episodes in the Gospels. Consider the conflicts about Sabbath observance. The opponents of Jesus insist that the Sabbath is the day reserved strictly for the honor of God. Even deeds of helping the needy are declared by some to be forbidden on the Sabbath. Jesus contends, on the contrary, that God is honored where humanity is set free. It is proper to do good on the Sabbath because "the sabbath was made for man, not man for the sabbath" (Mark 2:27). In this Sabbath debate as well as in the other conflicts of Jesus with his opponents, the central controversy comes to light—whether God is a power of repression and fear or a liberating force in the midst of life. The God whom Jesus calls "dear father" wants people to be free. Jesus empowers the powerless by extending God's forgiveness and affirmation to them. He tells the "nobodies" of his time that they are "somebodies" in God's eyes. This sense of worth and dignity is one of the greatest gifts of power that human beings can receive.

The freedom of the arriving Kingdom of God is a freedom *from* the bondage of sin and a freedom *for* service of God and fellow creatures. Jesus is no political revolutionary. He refuses to take up the sword in armed revolt against the Roman occupation forces. He does not form a political party to achieve social and political change. Nevertheless, his teaching and ministry are deeply disturbing to all existing power and authority. Jesus is viewed as a reactionary by the Zealots, who advocate violence to achieve independence. He is also seen as dangerous by the Jewish and Roman leaders, who are threatened by his message of a new kingdom of justice and freedom. Jesus turns accepted values upside down when he calls not merely for love of one's neighbor but for love of one's enemy (Matt. 5:43ff.). This runs counter both to the Roman reliance on brute force and to the hatred of the Jewish nationalists for their Roman oppressors. Thus Jesus brings about a revolutionary change in the meaning of power. While rulers of the Gentiles lord it over them, "whoever would be great among you must be your servant" (Mark 10:42–45). True power is not in domination of others but in service. The ultimate power is not mastery over slaves but the power of self-giving love.

The redefinition of God's power as extravagant and costly

love that wills others to be free is beautifully presented in
the parable of the prodigal son (Luke 15:11ff.). In this
parable a father allows his son to go off on his own. Having
squandered the family inheritance in loose living and
finding himself in abject poverty, the son has a change of
heart and returns home in shame. The awaiting father is
eager to forgive his son even before he is asked, and he
lavishes gifts on him. God's power, the parable teaches, is
not like that of a vindictive despot but like that of a caring
parent. This redefinition of the power of God creates anger
and resentment among those who hear the parable. They
react like the elder brother of the parable, who bitterly
resents the forgiveness and joy with which the younger
brother is received.

In this and many other parables Jesus describes the
extravagance of God's grace. It is his proclamation and his
enactment of the extravagance of grace—the surprising
inclusion of sinners, the undeserving, the unwanted, the
castoffs of society in God's Kingdom—that infuriates Jesus'
opponents. Jesus challenges their life world, their own
exercise of power, their personal and corporate interests,
which are tied up with their understanding of God's power.

In his entire ministry Jesus incarnates God's powerful
compassion and liberating love. The opposition which this
ministry creates eventually conspires to bring about his
death. Crucified between two political prisoners, he dies as
he lived—in utmost solidarity with the lost and despised of
this world. The meaning of Jesus' death cannot be rightly
grasped apart from his life and ministry. Jesus, the living
human parable of God's power, dies on a cross in faithfulness to God and to the cause of human salvation. The event
of the cross forever shatters the equation of divine power
with oppressive rule and self-aggrandizing mastery over
others. This is vividly expressed in one of the scenes of the
passion narrative. Those surrounding the dying Jesus mock
him with the words: "He saved others; let him save

himself" (Luke 23:35–36, 39). We might paraphrase these words as follows: "Show us that you have the power to save yourself, to survive, to look out for Number One, and then we will believe that you can also help us. For we want to survive above all else, and we acknowledge power that is useful to that end." The conception of power held by those who mock Jesus is exactly the bondage from which he wants to set them free. Their conception of power is totally self-centered. Jesus reveals the true power of God as self-giving love. He refuses to invoke the power of God in a way that would only support the dominant and dehumanizing ideas of divine and human power.

Among the New Testament writers, it is the apostle Paul who ponders most deeply the redefinition of the power of God brought about by God's presence and activity in Jesus of Nazareth. Paul knows well the coercive "power of sin" (Rom. 3:9) and the oppressive "reign of death" (Rom. 5:14) in human life. But God has shown his power in a completely unexpected form. A man crucified in weakness is the Lord. What to human eyes is shameful, weak, and ineffective is God's own glory and strength. This "weakness of God" (I Cor. 1:25) shown in the cross of Christ is stronger than all human might.

From New Testament times to the present the scandalous story of the crucified God has shaken to the foundations all preconceptions of divine power. The shock produced by the picture of a crucified Lord is movingly portrayed by the Swedish writer Pär Lagerkvist, in his novel *Barabbas*. At one point in the story, an overseer questions a Christian slave named Sahak about his faith.

"—The only God! And crucified like a slave! What presumption! Do you mean that there is supposed to be only *one* God, and that people crucified him!"

—"Yes," Sahak said. "That is how it is."

The man gazed at him dumbfounded.

The drama of the gospel thus requires a revolution in our understanding of the power of God. He who was rich became poor for our sake (II Cor. 8:9). God's power is "made perfect in weakness" (II Cor. 12:9). The powerful love of the crucified Lord is "the power of God for salvation" (Rom. 1:16), the power able to transform Paul himself from a persecutor of the church into an apostle, the power able to break down the barriers between humanity and God, between Jews and Gentiles, men and women, slaves and masters, the power that is stronger than death itself.

According to the proclamation of the New Testament, God raised the crucified Jesus from the dead. Jesus is not dead but alive by the power of God. The Spirit sent from God by the risen Lord is in the world today continuing the work that Jesus inaugurated. This Spirit of God is the power, the energy, of new beginnings in human life. The Spirit is the power of God at work among us, reminding us of the story of Jesus, breaking our bondage to self-centeredness and exploitation of others, and freeing us for a new life of inclusive friendship and community with God and with our fellow human beings. Where this Spirit of the Lord is, there is liberty (II Cor. 3:17). Where the Spirit is at work, there is the beginning of love and community in which each member is respected and valued.

To be moved by the Spirit of resurrection and new life is to undergo a conversion, a complete turnaround in one's understanding of power and in one's exercise of power. Nothing in one's daily life and practice is left undisturbed. The power of God present in Jesus and in his Spirit is the power of forgiveness of sins, of love of the enemy, of solidarity with the oppressed, of the passion for justice and reconciliation. God does not use brute force nor work by overt or subtle coercion. God is power that liberates by forgiving, power that builds friendship and new community among those once estranged, power that serves others in the daring hope of the completion of God's purposes for the

entire creation. Just as the Old Testament eagerly awaits a
new and fuller deliverance by the exodus God, so the New
Testament looks forward with utmost longing to the consummation throughout all creation of the new life in freedom and justice rooted in Jesus Christ and his Spirit.

If we are attentive to the New Testament witness, we will
discern a threefold pattern in its new image of the power of
God. This threefold pattern is the biblical root of the later
Christian doctrine of the Trinity. The central figure of the
new image is certainly the person of Jesus—his ministry,
cross, and resurrection. But the Jesus of the gospel story is
not an isolated figure. He is always related to the one he
calls Father, and he is also related to the life-giving Spirit of
God. We can summarize the New Testament witness in the
following way: God's power is made human in the person
of Jesus and continues to work through the liberating, life-
transforming Spirit. The activity of Father, Son, and Holy
Spirit defines the new shape of divine power according to
the New Testament.

God is the transcendent Lord who sends Jesus on his
mission of salvation. God is the humble servant who faith-
fully does the will of the Father and gives himself even
unto death that all of God's creatures might be free from
every bondage. God is the life-renewing and life-transforming Spirit that goes forth from the self-giving love of the
Father and the Son. The Spirit is the power of God's future,
the real pledge (II Cor. 1:22) and promise of God's coming
Kingdom. Thus the power of God—the power of creative,
suffering, transforming love—has a trinitarian shape according to the New Testament. God's powerful love is at work
in Jesus and continues to be present and active in the world
today through the Holy Spirit. The doctrine of the Trinity is
the effort of the church to express the revolution in our
understanding of the majestic power of God made known in
the crucified Jesus and his life-transforming Spirit.

4
THE POWER OF GOD
IN THE CHURCH'S THEOLOGY

The Attributes of God in Traditional Theology

According to the biblical witness, the power of God is different and surprising. The Bible describes this power in a way that shatters many of our assumptions. The power of God is not the power of authoritarian rule but the power of the exodus God who acts to liberate an oppressed people. The power of God is not the power of sheer almightiness but the power at work in Jesus' ministry—in his forgiveness of sinners, in his solidarity with the poor, in his suffering and dying for the world, in the continuing presence of his transforming Spirit who creates new freedom and builds new community. God's power is not exercised only in these events—but for the Christian community at least, it is here that we know what God's power, wherever exercised, is really like.

Some theologians have said that the history of the church is the history of the interpretation of Scripture. If so, we must add that this history has been one both of clarification and distortion of the message of Scripture. This becomes obvious when we trace what happened to the biblical understanding of the power of God in later Christian theology and in the life of the church.

In a note discovered after his death, Blaise Pascal, the great seventeenth-century scientist and philosopher, recorded the intense religious experience that changed his life. He provided few details of what happened other than to say it was like "fire." In this experience Pascal became unshakably certain of the reality of God. While Pascal was far from being a despiser of reason and philosophy, the God whom he knew with certainty in his fiery experience was "God of Abraham, God of Isaac, God of Jacob, not of the philosophers and scholars." For Pascal the living God is the God of the biblical witness: "God of Jesus Christ. . . . He is to be found only by the ways taught in the Gospel. . . . We keep hold of him only by the ways taught in the Gospel."

Pascal's contrast—even contradiction—between the God of the biblical witness and the God of philosophical reason touches an exposed nerve in the traditional Christian understanding of God. Many Christians through the centuries have felt the tension that Pascal experienced so acutely. In its theology and in its life the church has in fact moved back and forth between an image of God indebted primarily to the classical philosophical conceptions of absolute being and an image of God derived from the story of Jesus.

When the church expanded from its Palestinian beginnings into the Hellenistic world, the biblical message had to be expressed in new terms. In its articulation and defense of the faith the church made use of the classical philosophical tradition. The biblical story of God's creative and redemptive activity was expressed in categories used by classical philosophy to define the nature of ultimate reality. In this process the church both gained and lost. The gain was twofold. First, the philosophical categories were familiar. This made it easier for the church to communicate its teaching in an understandable form. Second, classical philosophy enabled the church to express the universality of God's lordship. By speaking of God in such terms as "Pantocrator"—the power that controls all things—the church prevented its witness from becoming the story of a tribal or provincial deity. Thus the early church cannot be faulted for appropriating classical philosophy or for using its categories to express the universal lordship of the God of the biblical witness. However, the question remains whether this appropriation was sufficiently critical. Did the philosophical categories that were employed as a help in understanding the biblical witness become increasingly a hindrance?

The negative results are seen most clearly in scholastic theology. By "scholastic theology" I mean those forms of Christian theology, both Roman Catholic and Protestant, in which abstract speculation about God leads to severely one-sided and distorted concepts of the God of the biblical witness. How did scholastic theology speak of God? What attributes of God were considered most important? According to scholastic theology, our knowledge of God is indirect and must proceed primarily by the ways of negation and eminence. We know God indirectly by *negation* when we recognize that God is not anything creaturely or finite. God is not finite (in-finite), not mortal (im-mortal), not visible (in-visible), not changeable (im-mutable). We know God indirectly by the method of *eminence* when we begin with the virtues found in creatures and then ascribe the highest degree of these virtues to God. Thus God is not only wise but all-knowing (omniscient), not only good but the supreme good *(summum bonum)*, not only powerful but all-powerful (omnipotent). A third way of knowing God, according to scholastic theology, is the way of *analogy*. Analogy combines negation and eminence. There is both likeness and difference between the attributes of creatures and the attributes of God. To speak of God as father or mother is to speak analogically. These traditional ways of speaking of God are helpful and even unavoidable. But separated from the biblical story, they fall short of a genuinely Christian understanding of God.

We find the influence of scholastic descriptions of God in some familiar hymns, of which the following is typical:

> Immortal, invisible, God only wise,
>   In light inaccessible hid from our eyes.
> Most blessed, most glorious, the Ancient of Days,
>   Almighty, victorious, thy great name we praise.

This hymn goes on to speak of God as beyond every want and as immune to all change. While the hymn contains some truth, the impression of the majesty of God that it leaves is very one-sided. The attributes of God that the hymn stresses tend by themselves to obscure the personal God of the biblical witness who acts and suffers to free people from sin and oppression.

Let us consider a few of the attributes of God as defined by scholastic theology. Most important is the attribute of *omnipotence.* In the Apostles' Creed the church confesses its faith in God the Father "Almighty." It is God the Father of our Lord Jesus Christ who establishes the true meaning of almighty or omnipotent. For scholastic theology, however, omnipotence means simply all-powerfulness. God is able to do anything, except what is self-contradictory. While God cannot create a round square or make two plus two equal five, all conceivable power belongs to God. Abstracted from the gospel story, omnipotence means simply godalmightiness. The power of God is the greatest power imaginable. This approach to the meaning of the power of God encourages a quantitative way of thinking. A child has a little power; an adult has more power; a king has a huge amount of power; God has the most power of all.

The biblical witness does not speak of God's power in this way. It describes God's power in stories of judgment and salvation. In the New Testament the decisive depiction of the power of God is the story of the passion and resurrection of Christ. Scholastic theology loses this narrative approach of the Bible and speaks of God's powerfulness in the form of abstract speculation about all the things that God can do. But the cross of Christ will not fit into a speculative scheme. It demands a complete overhaul of our thinking about power. God is certainly the supreme power. But this does not mean that God is "all the power there is," or that "God can do anything." Scholastic theology defines God's omnipotence in a one-sided, and therefore distorted, manner. According to the Bible, God has all the power needed to create, redeem, and complete the world in a personal way. The power of God made known in Christ is not sheer omnipotence but supremely powerful love.

Another very important attribute of God in scholastic theology is *immutability* or changelessness. The literal meaning of this attribute is that God does not move, or undergo change, or have a history. God is perfect, and what is perfect never changes. If what is perfect changed, it could only change for the better (in which case it was not perfect before) or for the worse (in which case it is no longer perfect). There is, of course, important truth in the affirmation of God's changelessness. God is not fickle. God does not have an unstable character. God is completely steadfast and faithful in character and purpose. This is the change-lessness of God that the Bible has in mind when it affirms that Jesus Christ is "the same yesterday and today and for ever" (Heb. 13:8).

Nevertheless, in some respects God does change. God does different things and experiences new things in interaction with the world. Just as we may engage in different activities as we pursue a single goal, so God does new things for the salvation of the world while remaining the same in character and purpose. Thus the idea of God as absolutely unchanging is a distortion of the biblical witness. Nowhere is the failure of theology to correct its philosophical inheritance in the light of the biblical story more evident than in the doctrine of the immutability of God. Whereas Scripture affirms that God has a purpose and remains faithful to that purpose precisely by doing new and surprising things, scholastic theology gets bogged down in the argument that God is immutable in every respect.

Absolute immutability, however, is a definition of death. In Jesus Christ we see the perfect, steadfast love of the living God, not the immutability of a dead abstraction.

[A third important attribute of God in scholastic theology is *impassibility.*] God is passionless. God is free from all suffering. God acts on the creation, but is in no way affected by what happens in the creation. God is absolutely self-sufficient, entirely independent of others. God has no need and experiences no weakness. In short, God is totally invulnerable. The intent of these affirmations is clear. God is not the slave of unruly impulses. God does not have vulgar passions as do the scheming and adulterous ancient Greek gods of Mt. Olympus. Nevertheless, while supposedly an exalted way of speaking of God, the description of God as passionless collides head on with the biblical witness. Does not the God of the Bible have a passion for justice? Is this God not genuinely compassionate in response to the cries of an afflicted people? Is God not affected by their prayers of praise and lamentation? Has not God in Jesus Christ become radically open to the life of the world and become vulnerable to human sin and suffering? In the light of the gospel story, God is not impassible, but passionate, suffering love. If God is love, then receptivity, vulnerability, and suffering are not strange to God's being. God is free to love and thus free to experience the suffering of the world.

The elaboration of the attributes of God in scholastic theology seems at first majestic and impressive. But the resulting image of God is cold and distant. It is a picture of God miserably inferior to the God whose perfections are made known in Jesus Christ. When we compare the scholastic way of describing what God is like with the biblical witness, we experience the great tension which made Pascal declare: "God of Abraham, God of Isaac, God of Jacob, not of the philosophers and scholars. . . . God of Jesus Christ."

Traditional Theology and Our Way of Life

The influence of the classical philosophical idea of God—as absolute, omnipotent, immutable, impassible—has been enormous. It would be a mistake, however, to place all the blame for what happened to the Christian doctrine of God on the failure of theology to appropriate more critically the classical philosophical heritage. This explanation would be much too simplistic and much too idealistic. The role of self-serving human interests must not be ignored. As pointed out earlier, the development of theology and the life of faith are always related to the social, economic, and political realities of the time. These realities do not necessarily determine theology, but they definitely influence it. Thus it is always appropriate to ask whose interests a particular theology is serving and what way of life it is informing.

In the early church the interests of the weak, the powerless, and the poor were central. Jesus preached good news to the poor. His proclamation and ministry shook the religious and political authorities. The apostle Paul reminded the Christians at Corinth that their community was not made up of the wise or the powerful (I Cor. 1:26). Many of the early Christians were uneducated and marginal people.

From the time of Constantine (fourth century A.D.), when Christianity was recognized as the official religion of the Roman Empire, the church and its theology were increasingly tempted to serve the interests of the wealthy and the mighty. This shift is reflected in the history of Christian art. In earliest Christian art the incarnate Lord is represented as a shepherd who cares for his sheep. The image of God as a shepherd is an image of gentle strength and tender care for the weak. This image of God's strong love stands in sharp contrast to an understanding of God as sheer almightiness.

God's power is caring, saving power. In later Christian art, however, the shepherd image is replaced by the image of the heavenly monarch surrounded by all the symbols of imperial wealth and autocratic power. God is now the heavenly Caesar, wearing a crown of gold and surrounded by many court servants. Since the time of Constantine, the power of God has all too often been understood both by believers and by unbelievers as the heavenly counterpart of the power exercised by masters, kings, and Caesars on earth. When people picture God as a celestial Caesar, it is all too clear whose interests their theology serves.

According to the author of the book of Revelation, the church in Laodicea was in mortal danger because it congratulated itself on its own power and riches: "You say, I am rich, I have prospered, and I need nothing" (Rev. 3:17). Complacent attitudes and self-serving beliefs are very much in evidence in many churches in North America today. In his "Poem for Rich Churches," the black American author Langston Hughes expresses the deep alienation of poor people from all "rich and wondrous churches" and the God worshiped in them.

> Rich and wondrous churches
> Where glowing beauties be,
> You close your doors
> To the poor and black
> And have no place for me. . . .
>
> Oh, not your God
> And not your Christ!
> No! Oh, no! Oh, no!
> (My Christ prayed in Gethsemane
> And drank the cup of woe.) . . .
>
> Oh, rich and wondrous churches
> Rising to the skies,
> Each one of you is a costly tomb
> Wherein the true Christ lies.

As this searing poem shows, we cannot place all the blame for the decline in the church's influence and effectiveness in the world today on scholastic theology and its impoverished ideas of God. We can say, however, that there is an all-too-easy partnership between an unexamined theology and a sub-Christian way of life. The scholastic theology still prominent in many places fails to challenge our way of life and our everyday priorities. It does not call in question those social and economic interests of the church and of individual Christians which are indebted far less to the gospel than to the images and standards of our competitive, consumer society. We shirk our Christian responsibility if we do not ask whose interests are served today by the images of God that inform the sermons we preach or hear, the church budgets we vote on, the church school programs we organize or attend.

We must dare to question prevailing views of the power of God. How does our understanding of the omnipotence of God filter down into our everyday practice? Do we in fact equate power with control and mastery over others? Is this, for example, the actual understanding of power that lies behind the way our denomination or our local church is governed? Do we assume that power in the church should be concentrated in one person or in one central committee? Do we think that men have the God-given power and right always to exercise authority over women? How does the everyday government of our churches reflect our view of the power of God whom we worship? And what witness does this form of governance in the Christian community make to the larger human community about the nature, distribution, and exercise of power? Is the governance of the church a witness to democracy or to authoritarian rule?

Or to take another example, how do our methods of evangelism express our understanding of the power of God? Do we employ a hard-sell technique? Are we abusive and coercive in our efforts to communicate the gospel? Do we respect the traditions and cultural heritages of other people? Do we measure our "success" as a church by membership rolls and budget figures?

We must have the courage to question our assumptions about the relationship between God and change. What are we really saying when we call God immutable or unchangeable? And how does this affect our attitudes toward change in the church and in society? Are we afraid of change? Do we think that everything would really be splendid if nothing ever changed? Do we long for the old-time religion when what was right and what was wrong were absolutely clear (or so we suppose)? Do we want a church where doctrines and ethical teachings remain as absolutely immutable as we suppose God to be? And if we want immutability in our religious life, what witness do we bear to the larger society in which we live? Do we favor an immobile society, one in which everyone stays in his or her God-given place? Do we resent or even resist efforts on the part of people who are working for change in our society in the direction of greater justice and freedom for those now deprived and exploited?

We must learn to speak boldly of the passion and suffering of God. What do we mean when we speak of the impassibility or the passionlessness of God? Do we want an invulnerable God because we secretly crave invulnerability to the suffering and affliction of the world? Do we want a passionless God because we are afraid of our own passions or because we are disturbed by the passion of others for justice, freedom, and human wholeness? Does our belief in God set us in opposition to conditions of oppression and injustice, or does our belief in God, the impassible one, make us indifferent to these conditions? Does our faith in God prepare us to face up to real conflicts in personal relationships and in society, or does it obscure or ignore these conflicts for the sake of peace at any price? Does our understanding of God encourage us to be critical of all efforts whether crass or subtle, to legitimize authoritarianism, to justify exploitation of the poor and denial of human rights, or does our understanding of God dull our moral sensitivity, substitute fantasy for reality and apathy for the passion for new life in a transformed world?

These are hard questions. If we want to be disciples of Christ, we must have the courage to ask them. The pilgrimage of faith includes the continual examination of our understandings of God in the light of the gospel. That involves our asking whose interests our images of God are serving and what way of life they are supporting.

The Power of God the Creator, Redeemer, and Transformer

While traditional ideas of God as omnipotent, immutable, and impassible are dangerously one-sided, we cannot regain the biblical perspective by thinking and speaking as though God were ineffective, inconsistent, and sentimental. This is the mistake of some liberal theologians in their attempt to get beyond scholastic doctrine. Whereas scholastic theology exalts the power of God at the expense of divine compassion, liberal theology exalts the compassion of God at the expense of divine power. All of our images of God must be radically revised in the light of Jesus Christ the crucified and risen Lord. He is the central clue, the key analogy to a right understanding of authentic divine power and fruitful human power. Martin Luther King had the standard of Jesus Christ in mind when he said: "Power without love is reckless and abusive, and love without power is sentimental and anemic. Power at its best is love implementing the demands of justice."

If we describe the attributes of God on the basis of what we think God should be like, the result will be arbitrary. What we call God will be only our secret fears and sinful desires. A description of the attributes of God, if it is faithful to the biblical witness, will focus on God's covenantal love for Israel and decisively on what God does and suffers for the world in Jesus Christ. No theologian of the modern period has adhered to this principle more consistently than Karl Barth:

> We may believe that God can and must only be absolute in contrast to all that is relative, exalted in contrast to all that is lowly, active in contrast to all suffering, inviolable in contrast to all temptation, transcendent in contrast to all immanence, and therefore divine in contrast to everything human, in short that God can and must be only the "wholly other." But such beliefs are shown to be quite untenable, and corrupt and pagan, by the fact that God does in fact be and do this in Jesus Christ.

In the light of the New Testament story the power of God is not a general and vague omnipotence. It is divine power present decisively in Christ and in his Spirit. The gospel story redefines the power of God. It is what God the Father does in giving his Son for the salvation of the world. It is what the Son of God does in graciously reaching out to include the sinful and the poor in God's Kingdom and finally in giving his life on the cross to reconcile all things to God. It is what the Spirit of God does to enliven and transform all who trust in him. God is Creator, Redeemer, and Transformer of life—not mere almightiness but creative power; not impassive but compassionate power; not immutable but steadfast, life-giving power that liberates and transforms the world.

We confess God as our *Creator*. The idea of the creation of the world conjures up the thought of an enormous exercise of power. Can we even begin to imagine the power released in the creation of the universe? Our universe with all its galaxies and countless stars had its origin in a powerful event of unimaginable dimensions. In contrast to such unthinkable power, whatever power human beings possess seems puny and insignificant. We are radically dependent on the stupendous power of the Creator. Thinking about God the Creator in this way may lead to a salutary recognition of human limits and may contribute to a spirit of humility. But there are also possibilities of serious distortion in this way of thinking. For the primary mark of God's power is not its massiveness but its creativity. And far from being aimless and destructive, creative power is purposeful and beneficial.

Creative power always involves discipline and self-restraint on the part of the creator. This is seen in the activity of all good parents and in the work of every artist. A sculptor respects the qualities of the material he shapes. A novelist allows the characters in her novel to have their own personality and independence. These are faint analogies of the creative power of God. In creating the world, God brings other beings into existence. The Creator does not hoard but shares power to live and to love. The power of God the Creator is empowering power. According to the Genesis story of creation, God gives people a share in the dominion over the earth. Creation is not a whimsical display of almightiness. The world is not the result of the sheer self-assertiveness of deity. God does not begrudge existence and power to creatures. As an act of letting another exist and of sharing power with this other, creation is an act of love and, like all love, involves self-limitation. Thus the gracious power of God manifest in the cross of Jesus Christ is not an altogether different power from that exercised by the Creator; the cross is the climactic expression of God's creative power.

We confess God as our *Redeemer.* In Jesus Christ we know God as compassionate power. God is not indifferent to creation and its destiny. God cares passionately for the world. Unlike the God of deism, the God of the biblical witness does not remain aloof toward and unaffected by the sin and suffering of creatures. God freely creates the world and freely suffers for the sake of its redemption. This compassionate power of God is perfectly embodied in the person and work of Jesus Christ. Compassionate power is not sheer powerlessness any more than it is sheer almightiness. It is stronger than sin and death. Weak if measured by the standards of compulsion, the compassionate power of God revealed in the cross of Christ is strong to save a world in bondage to self-centeredness, compulsion, and violence. From the sickness of seeking mastery and control over others, God can save us only by the exercise of a wholly different kind of power—the power of suffering love.

We confess God as our *Transformer*. In the power of the Spirit, the giver of new life, we are transformed into the image of our Creator and Redeemer. The power of the Spirit is not bombastic, sensational, show-off power. Neither is the power of the Spirit self-aggrandizing. Such power would not be renewing and transforming. It would not liberate us from the various bondages we experience. The power of the Spirit unites us to the gracious, self-limiting, and other-regarding power of our Creator and Redeemer. The power of God the Holy Spirit is anything but immutable. Immutable means motionless; the Spirit is in constant motion to further human transformation and to bring the whole creation to completion in God's Kingdom of justice and peace. Immutable means lifeless; the Spirit is the power of new life. Immutable means changeless; the Spirit is the power of repentance, conversion, and new beginning, the power that changes everything.

Christians do not sing praises to the absolute of the philosophers. They sing, "All hail the power of Jesus' name." Christians do not proclaim the story of Superman or Superwoman. They tell the story of Jesus, the Suffering Servant, whose power is entirely different from the principalities and powers of a world in bondage. Christians do not pray and baptize in the name of the Omnipotent, the Immutable, the Impassible. They pray and baptize in the name of the Father, the Son, and the Holy Spirit, and to this living God they sing:

> Praise God, from whom all blessings flow;
> Praise him, all creatures here below;
> Praise him above, ye heavenly host:
> Praise Father, Son, and Holy Ghost.

5
THE POWER OF GOD
WHO IS LOVE

The Meaning of the Doctrine of the Trinity

For many Christians the doctrine of the Trinity is the most obscure and confusing teaching of the church. The talk of God as "three persons in one essence" seems to defy logic and common sense. Of all Christian teachings about God, this one seems to be the least illuminating and the least significant for everyday Christian faith and practice. This is a feeling shared not only by laypeople but by many clergy as well. The story is told of a pastor who faced the task of preaching on Trinity Sunday with much misgiving. He solved his problem by informing his congregation that the Trinity was such a great mystery that in honor of it there would be no sermon that morning!

Despite these widespread feelings, the doctrine of the Trinity represents the distinctively Christian understanding of God. The trinitarian understanding of God pervades Christian prayer and worship. We baptize in the name of the Triune God (Matt. 28:19). We bless in the name of the Triune God (II Cor. 13:14). We sing praises to the Triune God:

> Holy, holy, holy,
> Merciful and mighty,
> God in three Persons,
> Blessed Trinity.

The doctrine of the Trinity is indelibly stamped on Christian creeds, liturgy, hymns, and prayers. And it is, after all, in our worship and prayer that we express our deepest convictions about God.

In an earlier chapter we pointed out that the New Testament witness to the reality and power of God is implicitly trinitarian. Jesus Christ, his ministry, death, and resurrection, is the center of the New Testament message. Yet the person and work of Jesus cannot be rightly understood apart from his relationship to God the Father, the Creator of the universe, who sent him on his redemptive mission. Nor can this person Jesus be properly understood apart from his relationship to the life-giving, transforming Spirit of God now at work in the world and among us. The gospel story in its fullness leads us to think of God in trinitarian terms. God the Father so loved the world that he gave his only Son to redeem it (John 3:16); Jesus Christ the Son of God became a humble servant and emptied himself even unto the abyss of death on a cross for our salvation (Phil. 2:5ff.); the Spirit of resurrection power (Rom. 8:11) who comes from the Father and the Son moves freely throughout the world to renew and transform it into God's Kingdom of freedom, justice and peace.

Thus the doctrine of the Trinity is not the result of murky thinking. It is simply the effort of the church—in language inevitably inadequate—to affirm what God is really like in the light of God's unique presence in Jesus the crucified and risen Lord and in the coming of the Holy Spirit. We do not engage in wild speculation when we call God Triune. On the contrary, we simply confess that God has been revealed to us in this way—as a Trinity of self-giving and other-affirming love.

A crucial issue involved in the development of the doctrine of the Trinity is the question of the nature of God's power. Is the kind of power at work in Jesus the ultimate power of God? Or is the power of God the Father different from and greater than what is seen in Jesus the crucified and risen Lord? At the Council of Nicaea in A.D. 325 the church declared that Jesus Christ is of "one substance" with the Father. This affirmation was directed against a priest named Arius who wanted to reserve real divinity— ultimate power—to God the Father. Arius' Jesus was divine only in an inferior sense. The church rightly decided against Arius that to separate the ultimate power of God from Jesus would be to create an idol of the human imagination—the idea of sheer almightiness. This would separate ultimate power and redemptive power. When the church declared that Jesus Christ is of "one substance" with the Father, it reaffirmed its trust in Jesus who said: "Whoever has seen me has seen the Father" (John 14:9).

If the Son expresses the true power of God, the Holy Spirit represents this power in all space and time. Thus at the Council of Constantinople in A.D. 381 the church confessed the co-divinity of the Holy Spirit, together with the Father and the Son. The liberating and reconciling power of the Spirit is one with the power of the Father and the Son.

The doctrine of the Trinity represents a revolution in the understanding of the power of God. It is a revolution in faith and theology more momentous than the Copernican revolution in astronomy, the Einsteinian revolution in physics, or the American and French revolutions in politics. Christians do not worship absolute power. They worship that divine power narrated in the gospel story and symbolized in the doctrine of the Trinity. The power of God is shared power, power that makes for just and inclusive community. Here is a radically new beginning in our understanding of God and especially of God's power. Every previous idea of divinity and every previous understanding of human power must be thoroughly and continuously revised in the light of the supreme power of the Triune God.

When Christians confess their faith, using the Apostles' Creed or the Nicene Creed (the most widely accepted creeds of the church), they affirm a trinitarian faith in "God the Father Almighty," in "Jesus Christ his only Son our Lord," and in "the Holy Spirit, the Lord and Giver of life." According to trinitarian faith, it is not a vague God in general—and certainly not raw power—that Christians acknowledge as Creator of the world, but "God the *Father* Almighty," God who is the Father of Jesus Christ our Lord. Similarly, it is not spiritual vitality in general or religious ecstasy of whatever kind that Christians confess as the life-giving, transforming presence and power of God with us here and now. Rather, the Holy Spirit is the renewing power of God that comes from the loving Father through his Son Jesus, who suffered and died for us. Where the Spirit of the Lord is, people are free to love God and each other and in this way begin to take part in God's own majestic love for the world.

Recent theology has reaffirmed the central importance of the doctrine of the Trinity for Christian faith and life. Influential theologians such as Jürgen Moltmann and Karl Rahner have shown the profound meaning and relevance of this long-neglected doctrine. They have argued that while the doctrine of the Trinity points to a great mystery, it is not nonsense. It is not an urge to speculate but faithfulness to the whole gospel story which leads us to speak of God in this way. Although we can never exhaust the mystery of the Trinity, we can grasp something of its meaning.

In the first place, the doctrine of the Trinity expresses the fact that Christians experience the one God as a dynamic and differentiated reality. The one God is the faithful Father, the servant Son, and the enlivening Spirit. The doctrine of the Trinity wants to say that these different ways in which God relates to us are rooted in the eternal being of God. The being of God is not lifeless uniformity. God is not mere mathematical oneness. There are real differences

within the living unity of God. Difference is the necessary
condition of genuine love. If we have a superficial or
sentimental view of love, we are prone to think that it is
threatened or even destroyed by differences. The love of
the Triune God, however, is strong and deep enough to
affirm and celebrate real differences in God's own life, in
God's relationship to the world, and among the manifold
creatures of God. Fear of differences among our fellow
creatures—whether racial, sexual, or cultural—may finally
betray an understanding of God as utterly monotonous. The
trinitarian vision of God opposes the destructive anxiety
that drives us to reduce all personal, social, and political
existence to a deadening uniformity, as happens in totalitarian movements such as Nazism and the Ku Klux Klan.

Second, God's triune being is communal or social in
nature. God does not affirm difference merely for its own
sake. God affirms difference for the sake of community, for
the sake of friendship and mutual love. Friendship and love
are given and received by those who are different, yet
whose love binds them together without dissolving their
differences. God is not the will-to-power but the will-to-
community in freedom. God is not absolute force that
crushes all opposition but the power of coexistence, the
will to be with and for others, the spirit of solidarity which
creates and sustains community. Community means persons in free, reciprocal, affirming relationship with each
other. On the one hand, we can never be persons in total
solitude and absolute independence but only in relationship and community. On the other hand, real community
exists only as persons are respected and loved in their
particularity and distinctiveness rather than being required
to conform to some abstract principle of unity. God is the
source of inclusive community. As Father, Son, and Spirit,
God exists in relationship. God exists as three persons
profoundly united in interpenetrating love.

Third, the mystery of the Trinity means that God is the

power of self-giving love. This is the deepest meaning of God's being-in-relationship. This is what decisively marks off the living God from the dead idols. They cannot give life because they cannot love. They cannot love because they cannot enter into communion with and freely suffer for another. The true God is alive and gives life to others. God is not turned in upon self. God is Spirit that goes out to another in love and thus brings forth new life. As the Spirit of self-communicating love, God is open to suffering for the sake of the beloved. From all eternity God is defined by this self-giving action, by this movement of the Spirit. For this reason it is possible to say that in the eternal life of God there is a readiness for the creation of the world and for the incarnation and suffering of Jesus Christ for the world's salvation. The coming of the Son of God and his sacrificial death on the cross are not chance happenings, not out-of-character gestures on God's part. The self-giving love of God for the world expressed in Christ and made present by the Spirit is consistent with God's eternal triune being. In creating and redeeming the world, the eternal love of God is extended outward. God's liberating and reconciling activity in the world is grounded in and corresponds to God's own eternal life of self-giving love. God does not have to create or redeem this world. These are free rather than necessary acts of God. Nevertheless, because God is the Triune God—the God who is love (I John 4:8)—we know that this God is eternally open, ready, and eager for deep and costly relationship with the world.

The Trinity and Human Suffering

If the Trinity is the deepest mystery of God, the immensity of suffering—especially the suffering of the innocent— is the greatest mystery of human life. Unless we can see a relationship between these two mysteries, faith in God will always appear abstract and removed from life. As long as

God is imagined as the absolute—omnipotent, immutable, impassible—no connection can be seen between the mystery of God and the mystery of human suffering. Such a God, however, is not the God known as Father, Son, and Holy Spirit in the gospel and in the worship of the church.

The mystery of suffering and evil is familiar to the biblical witness and to believers of every age. Why does God allow so much suffering in the world? Why does God allow innocent children to die of hunger? Why did God allow Nazi executioners to machine-gun their helpless victims or murder them in gas chambers?

In the novel *Sophie's Choice,* William Styron describes the horrible experience of Sophie, a Polish Catholic mother of two young children, upon their entering the concentration camp at Auschwitz. A Nazi commandant orders the mother to choose which child she will keep and which will be sent to the gas chamber. It is an unspeakably diabolical choice. Forced to choose in order to save one child, Sophie loses her faith in God and very nearly her sanity. The commandant, we are told, considered the choice he offered quite generous; after all, he had the power to take both children.

In the twentieth century the horrors of concentration camps and the atrocities of modern warfare have made it not only intellectually difficult but also morally reprehensible to believe in the omnipotent God of much traditional theology. What shall we say if God is able to stop all the carnage of history and refuses to do so? Is God then a monster? In a happier age it was possible for a Christian poet to write:

> God's in his heaven—
> All's right with the world!

After the glow and stench of the ovens at Auschwitz, such an expression of faith no longer seems believable or even honest. Many persons, both inside and outside the church,

would now find much more convincing the hard choice
posed by Satan in Archibald MacLeish's play *J.B.*:

> If God is God, he is not good.
> If God is good, he is not God.
> Take the even, take the odd.

Numerous attempts have been made by theologians to
defend God's goodness in the face of the reality of suffering
and evil (an effort called theodicy). One such attempt
declares that the evil which human beings experience is
entirely the result of the misuse of human freedom. If men
and women are to be free agents rather than mere puppets,
God must permit evil events to happen. Suffering is the
unavoidable result of the creation of a world in which
human beings have the capacity to turn away from God and
from their fellow creatures. According to another argument,
suffering is to be interpreted as a form of divine judgment
and as a stern call to repentance and a new way of life. Still
another argument is that suffering and evil can be put to a
good use. They provide occasion for spiritual growth that
would not otherwise be possible.

Such answers to the mystery of suffering and evil surely
possess a measure of truth. There are examples of all of
these approaches to suffering in the Bible, and we can all
think of particular instances in our own experience when
one or another of these responses might have been appropriate. But none of these proposals by itself goes to the
heart of the biblical witness concerning God and human
suffering. They fail to concentrate on the transformation of
the meaning of the power of God by the gospel of God's
presence in the suffering and death of Jesus. God suffers
freely for the salvation of others—that is the deepest message of Scripture regarding human suffering.

Dietrich Bonhoeffer was a young theologian martyred by
the Nazis. In a famous and provocative note written in his
prison cell, he declared: "Only a suffering God can help."

Only a God who knows the suffering and affliction of the human race to the utmost limits can help us. Only such a God can liberate us from our monstrous corruption of power, can reconcile us to God and to our fellow creatures, can promise new life in the midst of death.

Adolfo Pérez Esquivel, an Argentine Roman Catholic artist and winner of the Nobel Peace Prize, has given us a contemporary image of the suffering God in a painting entitled *Christ of the Poncho.* Leader of an ecumenical group that works with the poor of Latin America, this artist has depicted Christ in a poncho, the garment that is worn by peasants when the cold descends on the Andes or the rains deluge the tropical forests. The suffering God is present wherever there is affliction or need.

The suffering God is the Triune God. Only the trinitarian understanding of God consistently and unambiguously affirms that God, the Creator and Lord of all, experiences the deepest abyss of human suffering, abandonment, and death. The doctrine of the Trinity symbolizes what we know of God in the light of the crucified Jesus who was raised to new life in the power of the Spirit. The passion and death of Jesus are not God's punishment, anger, or revenge directed at an innocent human victim. On the contrary, the crucified Jesus is the unsurpassable expression of God's costly love for the world. As Jürgen Moltmann explains, all of the world's suffering is taken into the life of God on the cross. In the incarnation and its climax in the crucifixion, God the Father gives his Son to the world and experiences the grief of losing his beloved. Jesus' gift of himself is also an act of free, self-giving love. For our sake he goes through the horrible experience of abandonment by the Father and falls into the darkest abyss of separation and death. The Spirit of this costly love of Father and Son for each other and for the world radiates throughout the creation. The Spirit moves us to repentance and faith, creates in us a new freedom and joy, incites us to pray, encourages us to resist evil powers and to give ourselves in service to God's coming Kingdom of justice, freedom, and peace.

Thus the faithfulness of God to the world despite the reality of sin and misery is affirmed in the doctrine of the Trinity. In the light of the biblical story, we know that the Triune God is the God of suffering love who will finally triumph over all evil and death. God is the Father who sends his Son and grieves over his loss; God is the Son who cries out in affliction on the cross; God is the Spirit who groans with the entire suffering creation for the coming of the glorious liberty of the children of God.

Does this reduce God to a helpless and pitiful deity? Far from it. In the first place, the Triune God *freely* suffers for the world in bondage to sin and death. God willingly shares our misery and bears the judgment we deserve in order to bring forgiveness, freedom, and new life. The God who is able and willing to suffer with and for us all is not a mere victim of fate or necessity but the sovereign Lord of the universe. If God in Christ becomes a suffering servant, this shows both God's free grace and God's relentless judgment on all human pride and injustice. Thus in speaking of the suffering of God and of our Christian calling to take up the cross of discipleship, we do not imply that all suffering is willed by God. Instead, the message of Christ crucified reminds us of the great difference between suffering that is inflicted on others and redemptive suffering that is freely accepted in the struggle against evil. The suffering love of God does not sanctify the abuse of power; it places all unjust and cruel exercise of power under judgment. The suffering love of God not only moves us to gratitude for mercy undeserved; it also arouses us to resist all forms of injustice and oppression.

Secondly, the gospel of God's self-giving love does not end in complete tragedy and hopelessness. On the contrary, God's suffering love is victorious. This is the meaning of the confession, Jesus Christ the crucified is risen! The love of God is not ineffectual but singularly powerful. It is victorious in its own way. Jesus' resurrection from the dead is the promise of the ultimate triumph of the suffering love of God. The victory over sin and death is won not by force but by God's bearing the full brunt of evil. Evil exhausts itself in its opposition to that which is inexhaustibly good. This is the way in which the love of God wins its victory. The Spirit of the risen Christ liberates and transforms human life in the power of this love.

It would be a terrible mistake to understand the doctrine of the Trinity as a mere theoretical solution to the mystery of evil and suffering. Any attempt to "explain" the why of suffering may quickly fall into the trap of explaining it away. Suffering is not primarily a theoretical problem but an agonizing reality of life. Far from being an attempt to justify all suffering as necessary or good, the belief that God suffers with and for us speaks to questions that arise from the depths of human life: Is God completely trustworthy? Can we trust in God as our companion in suffering and death? Can we look to God as one who does not glorify all suffering but instead freely accompanies us in our resistance to and protest against absurd or socially imposed suffering? Does God call us to open ourselves in love to the costly risks of Christian discipleship, not because we enjoy suffering, but for a more just world, a world with greater freedom, a world of friendship and peace? These practical questions cannot be answered affirmatively if the God we worship is limitless, impassive, coercive power. However, we can respond affirmatively if the God we worship and adore is the Triune God.

The Trinity and the Coming Kingdom

The doctrine of the Trinity proclaims the distinctive power of God in creation, in redemption, and in the

consummation of all things. The Triune God is not only the
source of life, not only the power that judges and redeems
life from the bondage of sin and death, but also the power
that moves the world toward God's coming Kingdom. The
gift of the Spirit of Christ brings the "first fruits" (Rom.
8:23) of God's coming Kingdom of freedom, justice, and
peace. Led by the Spirit, Christians work and pray for
greater justice and peace on earth, but they do not confuse
these efforts with the final joy and glory of God's Kingdom.

How can we best symbolize the Christian hope for the
Kingdom of God? The biblical images of the coming Kingdom are numerous. It is portrayed as a time of peace and
harmony in all of the creation.

> They shall beat their swords into plowshares,
>   and their spears into pruning hooks;
>   nation shall not lift up sword against nation,
>   neither shall they learn war any more.
>   (Isa. 2:4)
>
> The wolf shall dwell with the lamb,
>   and the leopard shall lie down with the kid,
> And the calf and the lion and the fatling together,
>   and a little child shall lead them.
>   (Isa. 11:6)

The Kingdom is also pictured as a beautiful heavenly city
(Rev. 21:2), as a father's house (John 14:2), as a great feast
(Matt. 8:11), as a new heaven and a new earth (Rev. 21:1).
This is only a sampling of the treasury of biblical images of
the coming Kingdom. They portray in various ways the
completion of God's purposes, the total conquest of sin and
death, the end of hostility and war, the realization of perfect
justice and freedom, the final triumph of God over all forces
that spoil the good creation.

While we are familiar with many of these images, we do
not often recognize that the Trinity itself is a marvelous
image of hope, a beautiful symbol of life in perfect commu-

nity. In the life of the Trinity there is an eternal giving and receiving of love. Father, Son, and Spirit are different, yet united; perfectly free, yet perfectly bound to each other. Here is personal identity and freedom that does not destroy community; here is community that does not demand the sacrifice of personal identity and freedom. The Kingdom of the Triune God is the image of unsurpassed life in love, of perfect commonwealth.

The beauty and relevance of this trinitarian image of final fulfillment stands out sharply when it is compared with two other images of hope that struggle for the allegiance of humanity today. The first is the private utopia of autonomous individuals. Happiness is sought in self-realization, in the possession of things, and in the exercise of power over other people. Modern Western society—especially North American society—promotes this dream from cradle to coffin. Our national heroes are "self-made" individuals who have "lifted themselves up by their bootstraps." We expect businesses and corporations to pursue aggressively their own growth without giving much thought to the common good. We measure the strength of both individuals and nations by their achievement of self-sufficiency and independence. We are inclined to define freedom and happiness in terms of what we possess and consume.

Despite the emptiness and loneliness it produces, the drive to "make it" by oneself and to find happiness in private wealth remains the chief hope of fulfillment for many people in modern Western society. This utopia of individualism turns out to be more a nightmare than a pleasant dream. It elevates acquisitiveness and possessiveness over cooperation, friendship, and the cultivation of the common welfare. It confuses happiness with consumption, freedom with having many possessions, selfhood with solitary existence. However tempting it may be, the drive to possess and consume fails to satisfy our deepest human

longings. The fact is that we are made for community with
God and with others. Fulfillment cannot be found along the
path of individualism.

The second influential image of the future in our time is
the utopia that is built by military activity. This is the hope
that through revolutionary struggle and revolutionary violence a new world will be created. After the revolution,
freedom will replace bondage, justice will replace capitalis-
tic exploitation, peace will replace class struggle. If utopia
through private enterprise is the dream of millions in
Western societies, utopia through revolution is the dream
offered to millions in the Third World societies of Latin
America, Africa, and Asia. In some versions of revolutionary
utopia, everything and everyone must be ruthlessly subordinated to the revolutionary cause. The ends justify the
means. It is not the present but the future that counts. If
some people must be sacrificed now so that future generations will live in freedom, justice, and equality, the cost,
however great, is justified. This is a view of future community that betrays a disregard of actual persons here and now.
People are subordinated to abstract causes or principles.
Let there be no mistake: The Christian gospel itself contains a revolutionary ferment; it seeks continuing transfor-
mations of social and economic life to narrow the gulf
between rich and poor. The structures of the world that
keep many people poor and hungry must be vigorously
challenged in the name of Christ. But a new and inclusive
human community cannot be built by a spirit of vengeance
or a campaign of indiscriminate violence.

In *The Gulag Archipelago,* Alexander Solzhenitsyn de-
picts in frightening detail the systematic degradation of
human beings in the labor camps of Stalinist Russia. In the
name of the revolution and the creation of a new social
order, people suffered arbitrary arrest, the terrorist methods
of the secret police, separation of family members, impris-

onment without trial or appeal, and torture, exile, and death.

These two images of hope—the utopia of individualism and the collectivist utopia achieved by force—are equally destructive. Western societies contribute to the dehumanization of life by exalting individual interests at the expense of the common welfare. Revolutionary ideology contributes to the dehumanization of life by sacrificing persons in the name of abstract principles and ideals such as the classless society.

Trinitarian faith expresses a genuinely humanizing understanding of God and of the future to which all creation is called. We can hope and work, pray and struggle for the future opened up by the Triune God without being ensnared by either individualism or collectivism. The Triune God is being-in-community. Father, Son, and Spirit form a unity of interpenetrating love. The life of God is community in which differences are celebrated and love reigns. In the divine society power consists not in domination and control over others but in mutual giving and receiving. As Moltmann writes, "God is a Trinity because God is perfect love." It is to a sharing of this life and power of God in faith, hope, and love that we are invited by the gospel.

Thus the trinitarian understanding of God defines the power of God's coming Kingdom. It informs the Christian view of the fulfillment of human life and has profound political, economic, and social implications. It supports unequivocally an open and pluralistic church and an open and pluralistic society. It offers every encouragement to democratic as opposed to totalitarian government. It inspires creative efforts in the direction of a more just distribution of opportunity and wealth.

If the power of the Triune God is the power of community-forming love, if the Triune God enters freely into the suffering of creation for the sake of its renewal and completion, then not only the world but the very life of God has a history and a goal. As we previously noted, the Old Testament prophets announce the coming of a new exodus (Isa. 43:18f.). God will create a new heaven and a new earth (Isa. 65:17). God's justice and peace shall reign throughout the earth (Isa. 11:1–9). While the New Testament witnesses confess God's definitive action in Jesus Christ, they look ahead to the completion of God's purposes. According to the book of Revelation, the One who sits upon the throne promises, "Behold, I make all things new" (Rev. 21:5). Not even God already enjoys the new heaven and the new earth. God is not yet "everything to every one" (I Cor. 15:28). So great is the divine love that the glory of God will be complete only when the creation is free from all sin and suffering and free for everlasting life in friendship and peace.

6
THE RESHAPING OF POWER
IN CHRISTIAN LIFE

Faith in God and Self-Limiting Power

Does it make any difference whether we believe in God—
or more specifically, which God we believe in? Does our
understanding of God affect the way we see the world and
the way we view ourselves? Is it really important for our
everyday life and practice whether the ultimate power in
whom we trust is arbitrary and coercive—i.e., the spirit of
godalmightiness—or the powerful compassion of the Triune God? We have insisted all along that it does make a
difference, an immeasurable difference. The difference is
not merely theoretical but practical; it shows itself in the
way we think and act not only on Sundays but every day of
the week, not only in our worship and prayer but in our
business transactions and political decisions.

In this final chapter, I want to summarize the difference
faith in the Triune God makes in the everyday life of
Christians. Being Christian has often been described as a
life of faith, hope, and love. According to the apostle Paul,
these are the great and abiding gifts of the Spirit of Christ (I
Cor. 13:13). They are frequently called the Christian "virtues"—the powers of a new humanity made possible by the
grace of God. Faith, hope, and love are both *gifts* and *tasks*,
both *God's* doing and *our* doing. God's action and human
action are not mutually exclusive. The grace of God is

humanizing. It does not displace us or make us mere pawns. It calls us to new freedom and responsibility.

Let us begin with the virtue of faith and ask once more what it means to have faith in God. Faith is letting God be God. It is trusting in the power of God made known in Jesus Christ by his Spirit. To live by faith is to be relieved of the burden of "playing God." The God we seek to imitate when we "play God" is not God at all but the product of our fear and insecurity. When we trust in the living God, we are free to acknowledge our limits—to accept both our creatureliness and our need for forgiveness. In faith we are liberated from the desire to be omnipotent. We are freed from the fear that we must either use power to control others or be destroyed. When we live by faith we are able to recognize our limitations and to exercise self-limitation. Self-limited power is not the same as mere powerlessness. It is a reflection in human life of the creative and redemptive power of God that freely exercises self-limitation for the sake of life-in-community.

Healthy personal relationships require both self-acceptance and self-limitation. Both are rooted in faith in an accepting and self-limiting power beyond ourselves. We are able to accept ourselves because God accepts us in spite of how we are judged by others or even by ourselves; and we are able to limit ourselves because God exercises power in a self-limiting manner. Faith in God thus empowers persons for new life in relationship with others.

We can see the importance of self-limitation in family relationships. Family life becomes a tedious or savage power struggle if the members do not practice free self-limitation. One of every three marriages in the United States ends in divorce. Even more disturbing are the statistics that indicate that modern family life is all too often an ugly battleground. The large numbers of battered wives and beaten children are evidence of cruel and brutal power in the family sphere. The reasons for the crisis in modern family life are no doubt very complex. Nevertheless, it is clear that the popular philosophies of limitless self-realization and self-expansion contribute to the breakdown of family relationships. The future of the family in modern society depends on a recovery of the conviction that the ultimate power at work in our personal relationships and in the cosmos is a gracious, self-limiting power. Faith in God gives us the freedom and the inspiration to limit ourselves for the good of the whole. The yearning for omnipotence and absolute independence must be exposed as a psychological fantasy and a religious nightmare. If the God we trust in is the Triune God, we will acknowledge that true power is the power of life-in-community made possible by mutual self-limitation and mutual self-giving. God is not an absolute self but a God whose life is communal and who empowers new and lasting community among all people.

The practice of self-limitation, grounded in faith in God, is as important in the public realm as in the sphere of personal relationships. The grasp for limitless power—whether on the part of individuals or nations—is practical atheism. This is far more dangerous than any theoretical form of atheism. While some system of national defense is both necessary and legitimate, the quest for military supremacy quickly becomes idolatrous. Alan Paton, the author of *Cry, the Beloved Country,* tells of watching a passing convoy of military vehicles in South Africa. With sadness he comments that while many Afrikaners would claim to have a strong belief in God, they actually place their trust in tanks and guns. Are these Afrikaners very different from many Americans? Our coinage bears the motto, "In God we trust," but our soaring military budget loudly proclaims that our real trust is in large armies and sophisticated weapons.

The uncontrolled spread of nuclear weaponry has made the total destruction of human life a real possibility. In the face of a nuclear holocaust, the commitment to peacemak-

ing is taking on a new urgency both inside and outside the
churches. At the same time, allegiance to the gods of nation
and race severely aggravates the present nuclear arms
buildup. A former United States senator writes that some
countries are now at work on what they call an "Islamic"
nuclear bomb. This implies that there are thousands of
"Christian" bombs already in place in the United States
and Europe, thousands of "atheistic" bombs in Russia,
"Judaic" bombs in Israel, and "Hindu" bombs in India.
Can one imagine a greater blasphemy than to launch a
nuclear holocaust in the name of God?

Those who trust in God revealed in the crucified Jesus
must surely recoil from the mad race to produce and deploy
new nuclear weapons. If the God in whom we trust is a God
whose creative and redemptive activity consistently dis-
plays life-giving self-limitation, we are both authorized and
empowered to exercise self-limitation as a people. Recognition of the capacity for mutual destruction may act for a time
as a precarious deterrent to all-out nuclear war. But only the
power of self-limitation is strong enough to break the
vicious circle of the nuclear arms race.

Gestures of self-limitation in military policy are not a sign
of weakness but a sign of moral and religious strength. They
may also prove to be more effective than so-called "tough"
policies. Freeman Dyson, the noted American physicist,
points out that in 1969 the United States courageously
decided to abandon the production of biological weapons.
The Soviet Union was invited to make the action bilateral.
Negotiations were successful. Both sides recognized that
biological weapons were unpredictable and uncontrollable.
But it took the boldness of self-limitation on one side to
break the impasse.

The power of self-limitation is also crucial in our relationship to the natural environment and in our use of energy.
Western society has waged war on nature for many generations. For the sake of humanity and the whole of God's good

creation, this war must stop. If we trust in God, we will care for the natural order as God cares for it. God calls us to stewardship in our use of natural resources. This requires responsible exercise of power. To assault nature wantonly is a betrayal of the wisdom of the gospel. It is shocking to hear a public official say that he does not know for how many generations we should try to protect and preserve the national parklands since he is not sure when the Lord Jesus will return to earth. This is not an expression of strong faith but superficial piety used in the interests of the privileged few. God exercises creative self-limiting power in making the heavens and the earth and in freely becoming a humble servant for our salvation. Faith in this God will show itself in our time in the strength of self-limitation—in the conservation and responsible use of natural resources, not only for the sake of the present generation but also for future generations.

Love of God and Other-Affirming Power

According to the New Testament, "God is love" (I John 4:8). Christian life begins and grows in response to that love. Of the virtues of Christian life, love is the greatest (I Cor. 13:13). We are set free by the love of God to love God and others.

The conversion and transformation of human beings and their exercise of power takes time. Christian life is a journey. It is a movement from an old to a new way of life. It is a process of personal growth in relation to God and others. Like all growth, becoming Christian requires time and direction. God gives us time and patiently guides us on our hazardous pilgrimage. The patient power of God does not force our response. This is not to say that God does not bring us under judgment. But God's judgment is always purposive and intends to release us from self-centeredness to life in community with God and our fellow creatures.

Christianity is not a religion of solitariness but a social religion. This is plainly seen in the prayer Christ taught his disciples. When they pray the Lord's Prayer, Christians address God as "Our Father" and ask for "our daily bread," for forgiveness of our sins, for God to "deliver us from evil." The communal spirit of the Lord's Prayer is rooted in the gospel and ultimately in the very nature of God. The life of God is a social life. The òther-affirming love of the Triune God is the power and pattern of transformed human life.

Growth in Christian life always proceeds according to the pattern of the Son of God who humbled himself for our sake. The apostle Paul describes this Christ-centered pattern of Christian life.

> Have this mind among yourselves, which you have in Christ Jesus, who, though he was in the form of God, did not count equality with God a thing to be grasped, but emptied himself, taking the form of a servant, being born in the likeness of men. And being found in human form he humbled himself and became obedient unto death, even death on a cross. (Phil. 2:5ff.)

Christians are called to a life of service. They are called to take up their cross and follow Jesus. Christian discipleship is always costly. It is a life of self-giving love. Authentic love takes risks and is willing to be vulnerable. This willingness to risk ourselves for the sake of the gospel is part of the Christian calling. It will make different demands on different persons in particular situations. In no case, however, does bearing the cross mean making oneself a doormat. Christians follow the way of the cross, not because they glorify powerlessness, but because they find God's forgiving and life-transforming power in Jesus the crucified and risen Lord. They follow the way of the cross because they have experienced the costly love of God as stronger than all the powers of this world.

The risk of love for the sake of God's new community breaks the spell of narcissism that holds many people captive in our time. Narcissism is inordinate self-love. According to Greek legend, Narcissus fell in love with himself when he saw his reflection in a pool of water. Captivated by his own image, he refused to move for fear of losing his beloved. The myth of Narcissus describes one form of the human condition called sin. As sinners we are inclined to excessive self-love. We become preoccupied with ourselves or with those very much like ourselves.

Many popular movements today cater to this narcissism. These movements have found a home in many churches as well as in our society generally. We recognize power only if it enhances and expands the self. We are thus easily taken in by the latest movement or book or preacher who promises success and self-fulfillment. The beguiling slogans are all around us: God wants you to be successful! God wants you to have whatever you want! This is the message of modern narcissism, often cleverly packaged in references to the Bible and Christian proclamation.

Christian life, based on the power of God made known in Jesus Christ, contradicts this idolatry of the self. A character in Jean-Paul Sartre's play *No Exit* says: "Hell is other people." Nothing could be farther from the Christian gospel than this remark. In the light of Jesus Christ the truly human self is the person in relationship with God and with others. Our personal identity is to be found in open and inclusive community. Growth in Christian life is measured by an increasing ability to affirm the worth of others. Christian freedom is freedom to enter into solidarity with other people, and especially with other people who are very different from ourselves. The transforming power of God is at work in our lives when we begin to transcend self-interest and reach out in love and friendship to others. This is to be enlivened by the "Spirit of power and love" (II Tim. 1:7), to share in "the power of the resurrection" of Christ (Phil. 3:10).

The life together of a man and a woman can be a beautiful

sign of the power of God as it reshapes and works through human life. For Christians, marriage is not an empty social convention or a matter of personal convenience. It is a divine calling. It is a means by which God draws us out of life by ourselves into life in community. It is one important way by which the social personality of God is reflected in human life. Of course, marriage is not a divine vocation given to everyone. Being single is not a curse, any more than being married is automatically a blessing. Nevertheless, marriage and family life offer us a special opportunity to be shaped and to shape ourselves more fully into the image of God. The love of a man and a woman, and of parents and children, can correspond to the self-giving love of God in Jesus Christ. Marriage and family life can be a small but important expression of the life in loving community which God is and which God wills for us.

In his sermon at the wedding of Prince Charles and Lady Diana, Robert Runcie, Archbishop of Canterbury, said: "God does not intend us to be puppets but chooses to work through us, and especially through our marriages, to create the future of this world." God has given us "the royal task of creating each other and creating a more loving world." All couples are "royal couples" on their wedding day in that they are all called to help shape this world in love. "All of us are given the power to make the future more in God's image and to be 'kings and queens' of love."

What is true of God's working in Christian marriage is true of his working in the whole of Christian life. The gifts of the Spirit do not have as their goal a sense of superiority or self-congratulation. They increase our sensitivity to others, especially to those who are threateningly different from us—the handicapped, the poor, the politically or culturally oppressed, all those pushed to the margins of society for whatever reasons. Authentic Christian growth manifests itself in the readiness to be helpful in the building up of new, inclusive human community.

The church is essential for growth in Christian life because it provides the training ground of a new humanity. The church is far from perfect. It is not identical with the Kingdom of God but is a community of forgiven and forgiving sinners. The church is called to be the vanguard of the Kingdom, a community in which a new humanity is being shaped. Our human power is judged and transformed as we gather as Christians to hear God's Word, celebrate the sacraments of Baptism and the Lord's Supper, pray for guidance and help, and provide support and encouragement to each other. In worship we are drawn beyond ourselves. Our lives are redirected and our imaginations are renewed. We hear again the gospel story of the crucified and risen Lord, we praise the Triune God in hymn and prayer, and we express our trust in and love for the God whose life is open to us and who invites us to participate in this life through the work of the Holy Spirit.

The community established and sustained by the love of God in Christ is pluralistic. Christian community is not deadening uniformity. It is inclusive. It reflects and celebrates the diversity of life that God has created and redeemed. It corresponds to the richness of the life of God. Homogeneity in the Christian community is a contradiction of the gospel of God's powerful love, which frees us to accept as brothers and sisters those from whom we were previously estranged. A community that calls itself Christian and is complacent about its economic, racial, and cultural homogeneity is a community without the power of the Spirit.

Some church leaders advocate an outreach program for congregations that would focus on people most similar to their present members. But evangelism that deliberately aims at homogeneity for the sake of church growth is a display of impotence rather than real spiritual strength. The greatest of the gifts of the Spirit, according to the apostle Paul, is not some sensational power but the power of agape, the love that seeks out the different and the unwanted, the love that forgives and receives enemies as friends. Black and white, women and men, young and old, healthy and sick, are made one people by the love of Christ. As Paul writes: "There is neither Jew nor Greek, there is neither slave nor free, there is neither male nor female; for you are all one in Christ Jesus" (Gal. 3:28). Participation in Christian community should give us a chance to learn the day-to-day meaning of free and glad affirmation of people who are different from us. A policy of *apartheid*, official or unofficial, in South Africa or anywhere else, stands in contradiction to the open, other-affirming love of the Triune God.

Nourished and strengthened in Christian community, we are called to reach out in friendship and solidarity with all people, and always especially with people who are neglected and disadvantaged. The church does not exist for its own sake. It is not a closed circle for a select few. Christians are called to reach out to others, not out of weak pity, but out of the strong passion of the Triune God for a world of justice, freedom, and peace. Christian life is thus a practice of solidarity with the poor, the exploited, the victims of injustice. This is always the decisive test of whether the community that calls itself Christian is genuinely open to others rather than being turned in upon itself. It is a test more of right practice (orthopraxis) than of right belief (orthodoxy). If the power of God is liberating power, if it frees us to affirm others, Christians will want to express their solidarity with the poor and the oppressed. The Bible is very clear about this. We cannot love God and neglect or despise those with whom God has entered into utmost solidarity. On the Day of Judgment the Lord will not say to those who have been faithful: "You called me Lord every day." Instead he will say to them:

> "I was hungry and you gave me food, I was thirsty and you gave me drink, I was a stranger and you welcomed me, I was naked and you clothed me, I was sick and you visited me, I

was in prison and you came to me. . . . Truly, I say to you, as you did it to one of the least of these my brethren, you did it to me." (Matt. 25:35–36, 40)

Christian love is other-affirming power. That translates even more specifically into saying: Christian love is the power of solidarity with the poor. The first victims of every new upward spiral in the military arms race are the poor of the earth. The first casualties of every relaxation of commitment to human rights are the defenseless and the despised people in our own society as well as in other societies. The first human sacrifices of economic policies designed to make life easier for the rich are the weak and little ones of the world, those whom Christ called his brothers and sisters.

Christians will seek to share power with the weak and powerless of the earth. The just distribution of food and other necessities of life is an imperative of Christian love. Motivated by the Spirit of Christ, the church will pray and work for the responsible limitation of the power of the powerful and for the empowering of the powerless. The steadfast love of God is empowering power, power that liberates and reconciles, power that sets people on their own feet and calls them to shape the future together in freedom and friendship.

Hope in God and Future-Opening Power

The different power of God is the source not only of Christian faith and love but also of Christian hope. Faith is confidence in God that frees us from the destructive grasp for absolute power. Love is openness to and friendship with others, empowered by God, whose being is in self-giving and who is the source of all life in community. Hope, too, is a "virtue" or power of the new life in Christ. It is eager expectation of the transformation of all things by God.

To live in hope is difficult. It is much easier to live in

quiet or wild despair. When a crippling or fatal disease strikes us or a loved one, our understandable reaction is anger and resentment, and then perhaps silent resignation to our fate. When our efforts to assist downtrodden people in their struggle for justice meet with repeated failures, it is only natural and certainly easy to give up or to turn bitter and cruel.

Christian hope responds differently. It resists every repression of our yearnings for healing and wholeness in our personal life, and for justice and freedom in our social order. Christian hope fuels the passion for new life; it strengthens the longing for a new, transformed humanity in a redeemed world.

Christians dare to hope in the resurrection power of God which is stronger than all the powers of destruction and death in our world. Because the crucified Lord is risen and his transforming Spirit is at work in the world today, Christians boldly hope for the complete triumph of God over all evil, when the saying will come true:

> "Death is swallowed up in victory."
> "O death, where is thy victory?
> O death, where is thy sting?"
> (I Cor. 15:54–55)

This is the voice of hope in God which refuses to become resigned to the way things are, to say in despair: "What's the use? Things will never change." Resurrection hope holds to the promises of God which find their "Yes" in Jesus Christ (II Cor. 1:20). This hope enlists us in the struggle against all that demeans and destroys life. It encourages us to plead with God—even allows us to protest to God—to hasten the coming of justice and peace, to change what seems unchangeable, to redeem what seems a total loss. Christian hope keeps us restless for God's new world and thus allows no more than a provisional consent to suffering, loss, and death. The consent of hope is very different from resignation. In consent there is a refusal to give up and simply accept the lordship of injustice and death. Hope consents for the time being, for it dares to trust in a power that changes everything.

That power is the mighty compassion of God in Christ Jesus, whose transforming Spirit continues to work in human life and throughout the creation. The strong love of God is the unshakable foundation of Christian hope.

> Who shall separate us from the love of Christ? Shall tribulation, or distress, or persecution, or famine, or nakedness, or peril, or sword? . . . No, in all these things we are more than conquerors through him who loved us. For I am sure that neither death, nor life, nor angels, nor principalities, nor things present, nor things to come, nor powers, nor height, nor depth, nor anything else in all creation, will be able to separate us from the love of God in Christ Jesus our Lord. (Rom. 8:35, 37–39)

The powerful love of God shall be victorious. This is the reason we dare to hope for the completion of our incomplete and broken lives and for the consummation of God's purposes for the whole of creation. Because we dare to hope in God we refuse to go either the way of resignation or the way of retaliatory violence to achieve our goals. For resignation is hopeless, and violence only breeds more violence. Christian hope keeps alive and strong the struggle for justice and freedom. But it refuses to contribute to the spirit of revenge. Christians are called to bear witness to the "more excellent way" of love (I Cor. 12:31), even when with heavy hearts they believe they are required to take up arms to defend human life against outrageous injustice and brutality.

A distinguishing mark of Christian hope in God is its inclusiveness. In the first place, it embraces both the living and the dead. The Christian vision of the future does not regard the dead as mere stepping-stones to a future paradise built solely by human effort. The powerful love of God does not concede the final victory to death. As God raised Jesus the crucified from the dead, so God gives new life to all men and women of faith. Our hope is based finally not in ourselves, or in our social and political programs, but in the gracious God who brings into existence things which did not exist and who raises the dead to fellowship in the coming Kingdom (Rom. 4:17).

Secondly, hope in the "God of hope" (Rom. 15:13) embraces both human life in its totality ("resurrection of the body") and all of nature ("new heaven and new earth"). Christian hope is a breathtakingly inclusive hope rather than a small or partial hope. Neither individual souls nor even humanity as a whole exhausts God's plan of salvation. We hope in solidarity with all of our suffering and dying brothers and sisters. We hope in solidarity with the entire cosmos made by God and destined for transformation. Such hope makes an important difference in our everyday attitudes and practices. If we dare to hope not only for the living but also for the dead and those still unborn, if we hope not only for people like us but for all people, if we hope not only for the human race but for the whole of nature as well, we will repent of all petty visions of the future that absolutize the interests of a particular group. With the apostle Paul we will express our solidarity in hope with all of the groaning creation which restlessly awaits God's coming redemption (Rom. 8:21–23).

Possibly the most eloquent expression of daring human hope in this century is the speech of Martin Luther King, Jr., delivered in Washington, D.C., in August 1963 and entitled "I Have a Dream." King had a global vision of justice and peace. He dreamed of an end to racial discrimination and the exploitation of the poor. In his dream he saw a time when free men and women, of all colors, cultures, and national origins, would live in harmony with each other. The dream that King shared with millions of people and for which he struggled until struck down by an assassin's bullet was profound and moving. The "God of hope" inspires such dreams.

In contrast to the hope that expresses solidarity with all of God's creatures, there is a lot of narrow and escapist hope abroad in church and society today. Escapist hope makes doctrinaire predictions of the end of the world in the near future and describes this end in as terrifying a manner as possible. The narrow appeal of such hope is: Believe in Jesus and you will be one of the fortunate few who will be snatched to safety in the "rapture" when the horrible events of the final tribulation begin. These cocksure predictions that history will soon end in a worldwide nuclear holocaust, and this focusing of Christian expectation on the event of the "rapture," are distortions of authentic Christian hope. For one thing, Jesus himself denied knowing when the end would come (Mark 13:32). Moreover, Christian hope is not individualistic and self-serving as is the hope retailed by these prophets of doom. Christian hope is centered on the ministry, death, and resurrection of Jesus Christ for the liberation and reconciliation of the world. It hopes for the realization of God's justice and peace on this earth. Christian hope is not arrogant; it does not claim that God's Kingdom is identical with our efforts for a more just world. But neither is Christian hope escapist. It is well-grounded hope. It sees a beginning of the new world of God in the work of the crucified and risen Lord, and it experiences a foretaste of God's future in the presence of the transforming Spirit of Christ who frees people to live in new friendship and solidarity with each other. Christian hope is hope in the future-opening power of the love of God.

Rooted in the Triune God, Christian hope is nourished by images of peace and reconciliation rather than being fed constantly by images of war and death. Christians are called to hope, pray, and work for peace. They are summoned to seek peace among the nations, peace among the races, peace between the sexes, peace between humanity and nature. Peace can be realized only when the spirit of possessiveness is replaced by the spirit of creative, self-giving love, when individualism is replaced by the joy of life in community. Peace is not the mere absence of war. It is the dynamic and creative presence of life in friendship with God and others. Peace reigns where the spirit of the well-being of all triumphs over the individual will-to-power and will-to-possession. Christians live and struggle in hope for this peace and justice of the coming Kingdom of God.

A Christian trusts, a Christian loves, a Christian hopes. In and through all of these, a Christian will "pray constantly" (I Thess. 5:17). Prayer is a participation in the power of God. In prayer we give thanks that God's powerful compassion, embodied decisively in Jesus Christ and extended to us here and now by the Spirit, is greater than all the kingdoms and powers of this world. In prayer we ask God for daily bread and for forgiveness—for all that makes human life human. In prayer we refuse to accept injustice as inevitable, but we also refuse to use coercion to make the world change according to our timetable. In prayer we learn patience and wait on God. In prayer we receive new strength to continue the struggle for justice and freedom, for a more peaceful world. Thus is human power reshaped by the powerful love of the Triune God, to whom we pray without ceasing, "Thy Kingdom come," and to whom we gladly ascribe "the Kingdom, the power, and the glory forever."

QUESTIONS
FOR DISCUSSION

Chapter 1. THE QUESTION OF GOD'S POWER

1. What experiences of feeling powerful or powerless have you had that made you wonder about God's power?

2. Describe several "gods" from whom people today expect happiness and fulfillment.

3. What sense does it make to say that faith in God involves a continuous struggle against faith in the "gods"?

Chapter 2. IMAGES OF GOD'S POWER IN MODERN SOCIETY

1. What "anthropomorphic" images of God bother you or people you know?

2. Which of the three distorted images of God's power discussed in this chapter do you think is most widespread in our society today?

3. How do you react to the suggestion that there is a "partial truth" in atheism?

Chapter 3. THE BIBLICAL WITNESS TO GOD'S POWER

1. Discuss the claim that all of our knowledge of God comes from the Bible.

2. What conclusions would you draw about the will of

God for human life in the light of the Old Testament witness to the exodus of the people of Israel from bondage?

3. In what ways should our understanding of God's power be transformed by the New Testament witness to the life, death, and resurrection of Jesus Christ?

Chapter 4. THE POWER OF GOD IN THE CHURCH'S THEOLOGY

1. What questions do you have about the author's interpretation of the "omnipotence" of God as God's "supremely powerful love"?

2. To what extent is the way your local church is governed an appropriate witness to the way God exercises authority and power in Jesus Christ?

3. What is the importance of recognizing that God is receptive as well as active?

Chapter 5. THE POWER OF GOD WHO IS LOVE

1. In what ways has this chapter helped you to understand better the mystery of the Trinity?

2. Why do you agree or disagree with Bonhoeffer that "only a suffering God can help" us?

3. How might the image of God as triune influence our understanding of what it means to be a person and what the Kingdom of God is like?

Chapter 6. THE RESHAPING OF POWER IN CHRISTIAN LIFE

1. Give some illustrations of the importance of self-restraint in the exercise of power by individuals. By nations.

2. Defend or criticize the claim that the Christian calling

to affirm and love others means that we should be purely passive in our relationships.

3. How would you interpret the statement that "Christian hope is a breathtakingly inclusive hope rather than a small or partial hope"?

REFERENCES

In this volume reference is made to the following books and periodicals, which are listed in the order of their use:

Buber, Martin. "Power and Love," in *A Believing Humanism: My Testament, 1902–1965*, tr. by Maurice Friedman. Simon & Schuster, 1967.

Chapter 1. THE QUESTION OF GOD'S POWER

Gallup, George, Jr., and Poling, David. *The Search for America's Faith*. Abingdon Press, 1980.

Luther, Martin. *Luther's Large Catechism*. Augsburg Publishing House, 1935.

O'Connor, Flannery. "The Lame Shall Enter First," in *Everything That Rises Must Converge*. Farrar, Straus & Giroux, 1965.

Chapter 2. IMAGES OF GOD'S POWER IN MODERN SOCIETY

Anderson, Sherwood. *Winesburg, Ohio: A Group of Tales of Ohio Small Town Life*. Viking Press, 1958.

Calvin, John. *Institutes of the Christian Religion*, Vol. I, ed. by John T. McNeill, tr. by Ford Lewis Battles. The

Library of Christian Classics, Vol. XX. Westminster Press, 1960.

Hartshorne, Charles. *Man's Vision of God and the Logic of Theism.* Willett, Clark & Co., 1941.

Moltmann, Jürgen. "Introduction," in Ernst Bloch, *Man on His Own: Essays in the Philosophy of Religion.* Herder & Herder, 1970.

Chapter 3. THE BIBLICAL WITNESS TO GOD'S POWER

Lagerkvist, Pär. *Barabbas.* Random House, 1951.

Chapter 4. THE POWER OF GOD IN THE CHURCH'S
THEOLOGY

Barth, Karl. *Church Dogmatics,* Vol. IV, Part I, ed. by G. W. Bromiley and T. F. Torrance. Edinburgh: T. & T. Clark, 1956.

Hughes, Langston. "Poem for Rich Churches," in Jean Wagner, *Les Poèts Nègres des États-Unis.* Paris: Librairie Istra, 1963.

King, Martin Luther, Jr. *Where Do We Go from Here: Chaos or Community?* Harper & Row, 1967.

Pascal, Blaise. "Pascal's Memorial," in *Great Shorter Works of Pascal,* tr. by Emile Caillet and John C. Blankenagel. Westminster Press, 1948.

Chapter 5. THE POWER OF GOD WHO IS LOVE

MacLeish, Archibald. *J.B.: A Play in Verse.* Houghton Mifflin Co., 1958.

Moltmann, Jürgen. *The Trinity and the Kingdom.* Harper & Row, 1981.

Solzhenitsyn, Alexander. *The Gulag Archipelago.* 3 Vols. Harper & Row, 1979.

Styron, William, *Sophie's Choice.* Random House, 1979.

Chapter 6. THE RESHAPING OF POWER IN CHRISTIAN LIFE

Dyson, Freeman. *Disturbing the Universe.* Harper & Row, 1979.

McCarthy, Eugene. "The 1980 Campaign: Politics as Entropy," in *Christianity and Crisis,* Vol. 40, No. 13 (Aug. 18, 1980).

New York Times, July 30, 1981. (Excerpts from sermon given by the Archbishop of Canterbury at the royal wedding.)

Sartre, Jean-Paul. *No Exit and Three Other Plays.* Random House, Vintage Books, 1965.

BOOKS
FOR FURTHER READING

Barth, Karl *The Humanity of God.* John Knox Press, 1960.

Bracken, Joseph A. *What Are They Saying About the Trinity?* Paulist Press, 1979.

Cobb, John. *God and the World.* Westminster Press, 1969.

Cone, James H. *God of the Oppressed.* Seabury Press, 1975.

Kaufman, Gordon D. *The Theological Imagination: Constructing the Concept of God.* Westminster Press, 1981.

Küng, Hans. *Does God Exist? An Answer for Today.* Doubleday & Co., 1980.

Macquarrie, John. *The Humility of God.* Westminster Press, 1978.

Moltmann, Jürgen. *The Crucified God.* Harper & Row, 1974.

Niebuhr, H. Richard. *Radical Monotheism and Western Culture.* Harper & Row, 1960.

Russell, Letty M., ed. *The Liberating Word: A Guide to Nonsexist Interpretation of the Bible.* Westminster Press, 1976.